BIGFOOT

THE MINNESOTA SCENE

MIKE QUAST

HANGAR 1 PUBLISHING

CONTENTS

INTRODUCTION

I have been a Bigfoot researcher in Minnesota since finishing high school in the late eighties. From early childhood, I was always naturally drawn to any and all paranormal, supernatural, or generally wild and weird subjects, which came to include cryptozoology and the study of "monsters," with the big three being Loch Ness, Yeti, and Bigfoot. I doubt it ever would have become just a phase, but it was truly carved in stone with my own Bigfoot sighting while on a Sunday drive with my family at Strawberry Lake in a wooded area of Becker County, Minnesota, at age eight in the summer of 1976. It was fleeting —a ten-second glimpse of a large upright black creature perhaps 150 yards away standing beside a highway and then walking on two legs into the woods—but it made a powerful impact on me and ensured that wanting to learn more about such things and sharing them with the world would always be a part of my life. My parents and sister were also in the car, but I was the only one who saw it. Native Americans have told me I was the only one meant to see the creature at that moment and that it was invisible to everyone else. I don't know what to say to that and can only relate it as I was told.

During the late eighties and early nineties, I traveled extensively around Minnesota, becoming familiar with much more of my home state than I had ever been aware of in childhood, seeking out other Bigfoot witnesses and exploring wilderness areas for evidence, eager for another sighting. I grew up in a region of prairie, farms, fields, and pastures, without any real sense of just how much dense forest there is in the state. Now I know that the entire upper third of Minnesota is essentially one giant forest sporadically populated by small towns, and that the rest of the state has other wilderness areas here and there that are all excellent habitats for a huge, legendary, upright, manlike or apelike creature to dwell, if in fact such a thing actually exists.

During that pre-internet period, I did everything I could to research the history of Bigfoot in the state, knowing the creatures had first become known in the Pacific Northwest but that they had also been seen throughout North America to varying degrees. There was only a tiny number of Minnesota reports in books at the time, and I found only a few references to people who had made this same effort before me to document Bigfoot in the state. At the time, I seemed to be the only Bigfoot guy in Minnesota, and in reaching out to other researchers in the country I became known as that. I also corresponded with people around the world who began to have an interest in what I thought about things. I can't say I was famous, but I was known by a wide audience and proud of that.

I have always been inclined toward writing, producing an endless series of stories and comics as a kid. Now, in adulthood, it seemed natural to write about Bigfoot. For several years, I produced a newsletter called *The Sasquatch Report* that had many subscribers, and I penned a few self-published books that I published through local print shops, as I lived in the Fargo, North Dakota-Moorhead, Minnesota metro area. That was a fun time, but it wound down as the years passed and I got older. As we all moved into the 21st century, things changed. I began to hear of other Bigfoot researchers in Minnesota, some just individuals and others forming organized groups. This was exciting and gave me energy to keep going. Though new people had started gaining the spotlight, and there was a feeling of passing the torch, I never let a year pass without getting out into the field to look for Bigfoot at least a few times. Sometimes, other researchers mentioned my work, which was a great honor. Over the years, my research expanded Minnesota's few Bigfoot reports into a database of over 700, which I published in hopes of having an impact.

And it did. In 2021, after having resigned myself to becoming a background character in the field of Minnesota Bigfoot research, I got an offer to have all my previously self-published books produced in professional versions and sold online, so I was now a legitimate, published author. This happened amid new and exciting Bigfoot activity in the state and a nationwide Bigfoot renaissance. Bigfoot documentaries were all over TV and the internet, with Animal Planet's show, *Finding Bigfoot* front and center. That show filmed three episodes in Minnesota. Meanwhile, Remer, a small town in the Chippewa National Forest, started an annual festival called Remer Bigfoot Days based on the number of encounters in the area. Also, an annual Minnesota Bigfoot Conference began in Grand Rapids. I took part in all of this, and though fame was not something I had ever really cared about, my star did seem to shine again at least a little in this new era. People cared about what I had done, which gave me a great feeling of accomplishment and satisfaction.

Now, there is a small number of groups in Minnesota as well as a few individuals involved in Bigfoot research, and I am among them. I present this book in order to showcase each of them, to interview and let them tell their own stories. Not everyone invited to respond to questions did so, but enough did that I am able to present a good picture of the state of Bigfoot research in Minnesota. I should also mention that, while good friendships exist between some of these people, not all of them agree or get along. There have been arguments and controversies within this field, but that's hardly a new thing, as Bigfooters nationwide have a long history of discord despite having more in common than they have differences. This book will not cover that. In covering all the disparate groups and individuals, it will only present each on their own merits, showing their differences in their own words without judgement. As you will see, one major point of contention is whether Bigfoot is just a natural flesh and blood animal that is so elusive because of its high level of intelligence or some kind of paranormal entity.

Finally, the last chapter is to update my previous book, *Sasquatch Central: High Strangeness at a Minnesota Homestead*, which came out in 2021. This is by far the most intense Bigfoot case I have been involved in and feels like a reward for all my years of searching. It has made me seriously debate with myself the argument over the creatures being natural or paranormal. It's a rich and wild story, and I present it to all of you honestly and with the genuine observations of all the various people involved, which includes me.

I love my home state. Minnesota is a land of bitterly cold, stormy winters and hot summers. For what it's worth, it has produced celebrities such as Bob Dillon, Prince, and Jesse Ventura, as well as the Twins, who have won the World Series, and the Vikings, who just can't seem to conquer the Superbowl. It is a major agricultural center with endless farms, fields, and pastures, and has two major metro areas in the shipping hub of Duluth on the Great Lakes and the Twin Cities of Minneapolis and St. Paul, which, along with their suburbs, harbor over 3.5 million people. This is where there are huge expanses of forest, where deer, black bears, wolves, and even mountain lions (which officially are not supposed to be here) roam, and where the biggest concentration of bald eagles in the country soar through the skies. It contains the headwaters of the mighty Mississippi River, and in addition to its nickname of the "gopher state," it is known as the Land of 10,000 Lakes. It is not a perfect place, but it is a beautiful one that I believe to be one of the best suited states east of the Rockies to harbor the legendary Bigfoot.

As with most of the continent, there is a strong Native American presence in Minnesota that recognizes the existence of the creatures in their centuries-old folklore. The Ojibwa or Chippewa people, as well as the Sioux, have their venerated names for them: *Cee ha tonka, Memegwicio, Gitche Sabe*. These are powerful titles, all of which basically mean "big man of the wilderness."

I welcome you all to this book. I hope it is a fun ride.

1

MINNESOTA BIGFOOT RESEARCH TEAM

One of the most visible and publicly known Bigfooting groups in Minnesota is the Minnesota Bigfoot Research Team, or MNBRT, led by Abe DelRio of the Twin Cities area and comprised of members from throughout other areas of the state. In his mid-forties, Abe is a charismatic character who has built an extensive public presence for his team. Their black and green logo is emblazoned on clothing and other items they sell; at the same time, they conduct extensive fieldwork throughout the state in search of Bigfoot and investigate reports that come their way. One area they have a particularly keen interest in is the one around the town of Remer in Cass County, within the Chippewa National Forest. This town bills itself as "the home of Bigfoot" and hosts an annual Bigfoot festival called Remer Bigfoot Days on the first weekend after the Fourth of July, where Abe and his team are always a fixture, interacting with the public and giving presentations about their exciting experiences. Since 2020, Abe has also been the organizer and head of the annual Minnesota Bigfoot Conference in Grand Rapids in Itasca County about thirty miles north of Remer, which draws celebrity speakers from the Bigfoot field and large crowds of Bigfoot enthusiasts.

For me, it's amusing that while I first heard of Abe from other researchers in Minnesota, I didn't actually meet him until we were both attending the fiftieth anniversary celebration of the Patterson-Gimlin Bigfoot film in Willow Creek, California in October 2017. His ever-present MNBRT t-shirt stood out amid the crowd, and I thought that must be him, so I introduced myself, and we shared a laugh over how the two Minnesota guys had to travel half a nation away in order to finally meet each other. Three years later, when he was first starting to organize the Grand Rapids conference, he invited me to be a presenter in that first year, standing alongside nationally known Bigfooters like Cliff Barackman and Ron Morehead. That was a great honor.

Abe responded to questions for this book over time, between fall 2023 and spring 2024:

MIKE QUAST: Can you describe how you first got interested in Bigfoot and how this eventually led to you forming the Minnesota Bigfoot Research Team?

ABE DELRIO: I first got interested in Bigfoot by going to Como Zoo in St. Paul, because my parents would take me there as a young child. When my parents wanted to go to a different part of the zoo, I would throw a tantrum and not want to go because I was so fascinated and awestruck by the gorillas and how they looked so humanlike. That started all of this for me. Then, growing up and hearing about the occasional Bigfoot sighting coming across the news. The radios and the newspapers added even more fuel to the fires. I remember going to public and school libraries looking for Bigfoot books and thumbing through the pages and seeing the Patterson-Gimlin film and just becoming awestruck with that creature and thinking, there is a gorilla out there that walks on two legs.

It wasn't until the late nineties when I really started paying more attention to the Bigfoot subject and reading everything that I could. That was on the internet at that time and coming to my own conclusions that there is something out there that people are still seeing, and thinking there's something more to this. What are people seeing, not just in North America, but throughout the world, that is tall, hairy, muscular, big—that has big feet? I wanted to experience it. I wanted to see one and had some friends who were at least interested in the subject, so I established the Minnesota Bigfoot Research Team (MNBRT) in 2000 and started doing field research for myself with a couple of friends/team members.

MQ: Your team is very visible to the public with your logo displayed on clothing and various other items. What role does this play in your research?

AD: The Minnesota Bigfoot Research Team and Minnesota Bigfoot Conference logos are a form of identification, and we hope others recognize the logos. I mean, everybody knows McDonald's golden arches. I hope our logos will be recognized like McDonald's, not for food obviously, but because of our research. A research team that has great credibility. A team that has logged many hours in the woods, researching four seasons out of the year and has experienced many things from class A and class B encounters. We hope our logo is a logo that people seek out in hopes of relaying their stories, because they can trust our team and that we won't be making fun of them, and that we'll keep their encounter confidential if they so please.

MQ: Where have you found what you would call the best Bigfoot hotspots?

AD: The best Bigfoot hotspots, I would say, are in northern Minnesota. I know that's really vague, but as far as getting down to a pinpoint location, and due to ongoing research in areas, we like to keep a lot of this confidential and strictly within the team. But around the Remer, Minnesota area would be a good place to look.

MQ: Are there certain techniques you use in interviewing witnesses and in conducting fieldwork?

AD: In interviewing someone that had a sighting, it is highly important for them to be listened to, and for them to relay everything that they can remember. As a researcher/investigator, I realize that sometimes there may be some exaggeration or even lying, as somebody is trying to pull something over our eyes, so when I am interviewing a witness, I give them the opportunity to share all that they can, and while they are relaying their encounter, I am watching how their body reacts and how their eyes move and their mannerisms to see if there is any possible way that they are lying or fabricating it. For example, if the sighting of the Bigfoot really excited them or scared them, their body is going to react to the moment of the sighting, where their hair may stand up on their arms or the back of their neck, and goosebumps may be visible on their arms as well. Their breathing may become a little faster, and their speech too; whereas, somebody that is fabricating or making it up might just stand there and relay what their story is without any bodily reactions. They may not make direct eye contact or very little of it. So when interviewing somebody, I like to watch them and see how they react when they are telling the alleged sighting or what took place, because that would be a huge determiner of the credibility of the witness.

Another technique in interviewing a person who may have had a sighting is the questioning. Yes, I definitely want to help the witness in any way I can, but if you are not aware of how to question a witness, you may be helping them to fabricate by asking them leading questions. A leading question is a question that prompts or encourages the desired answer. For instance, if the witness is describing the Bigfoot's head, for example, and describing the shape of the head but really doesn't give it too much detail, and if a researcher were to say, "Was it pointed like a gorilla?" then your witness is more likely to say, "Yes, there was a point to the head much like a gorilla has." But if you give the witness a couple of options as far as the shape of the head, for example, "Was the head more like a human head and rounded, or was the head of the creature more like a gorilla and kind of had a point or a conical head?" then in that tactic of questioning you are helping them from their own memory to bring out detail instead of pointing the witness.

When it comes to techniques in the field, some think they know when you are there, and they might be right; however, when entering an area of research, I personally like to try to be quiet and very stealthy and have cell phones on vibrate instead of loud notifications and to try to walk as softly and quietly as possible. And I hope not to give up our location or make it known that we are in the woods if they already do not know. A lot of people like to wear camouflage. I don't think that really makes a difference. And I say that because of how many hunters have had a bigfoot come right under their stand, or have had some kind of debris thrown at them in their blinds. So, I do not wear camouflage.

As far as techniques, I think everybody knows by now about how great apes use wood on wood sounds for communication, and yes, we implement that when we are out researching and have had success by doing so. Another technique we use is vocalizations and have had success with that. In 2018, we were on a reservation in northern Minnesota, and a team member did what is known as the Ohio howl. We got coyotes responding, and then we got a return vocalization from where the coyotes were and then from a completely different location. Another Ohio howl was heard, and me and the team were in between these two creatures vocalizing, and that was a very amazing experience to have.

In conducting field research, one of the most important things is to be very self-disciplined, especially if coming across a possible footprint impression or sounds. This is because natural phenomena, such as animal tracks or weather effects, can create elongated and wide impressions that may resemble alleged Bigfoot footprints, and when it comes to sounds or vocalizations, I would recommend researching the wildlife. You have animals around that are native and local, and see if you can find a database on some of the sounds that they make so you can familiarize yourself with them instead of possibly jumping to conclusions when you hear one out in the woods, doing research, and saying that must be a bigfoot.

MQ: Can you recount some of your most memorable experiences in the search for Bigfoot?

AD: My very first memorable experiences while doing Bigfoot field research right off the bat would have to be my very first encounter in 2001 in Ohio. Me and two team members went there for our very first Bigfoot expedition. We found ourselves in Coshocton County in an area called Wills Creek. There were scattered rain storms on this particular day, and the sun would peek through the clouds from time to time. The three of us were in the general store there, and we told the employees who we are and what we're doing and where we were from. They asked us if we had been to Sasquatch Valley. It supposedly got its name in the seventies because of the activity that was going on then. Never hearing of it. They got a map out and showed us how to get there. We arrived, and an ex-team member and I got out while the other wasn't feeling well and didn't want to get out of the car. We parked the car facing the creek on the berm. We watch down the declining embankment, paralleling the creek, and we get to a distance of about fifty to seventy-five yards away from the vehicle, and right before we get to the heavier wooded area, we hear what sounded like a branch being broken or a tree being snapped. Was that sasquatch right in our tracks? And we listened. Then we heard loud movement that was undeniably bipedal footsteps walking on leaves and sticks. You could hear the debris crunching and cracking with every step that it took. We were very freaked out, and, of course, we were caught off guard, not expecting anything to happen. This was a very surreal moment. The ex-member was spooked and looked up at me, and I looked down at him, and his face was flush with color, pretty pale. We did not know at the time what was making its way towards us, but we decided to try to run back to the vehicle and ex-team member. And while attempting to run back to the vehicle, I had a Polaroid camera around my neck, and I stopped and flipped it open, focusing on the heavy footfalls and waiting for whatever was making them to make its appearance from the thickness of the woods. When I stopped and opened the Polaroid, the ex-team member who was in the vehicle was now out of the vehicle. I've known him since high school, and he is my blood brother. He yelled, "Abe! What are you doing? It's right behind you. Get going!" As he got my attention, I saw his face—eyes as wide as saucers and fear on his face—plus the sounds of the sticks and leaves getting louder. I closed the camera and started running back. Due to the heavy rain, the ground was very muddy, and the mud would accumulate on the bottom of my boot with every step. I had batteries in my pockets and no belt on, so in trying to make my way back to the car, my pants wanted to fall down, so I was running with a swinging camera around my neck holding my pants up high. Stepping through the mud, I was not too far behind the other guy, who was right by my side, and I believe we got to the car around the same time, and I don't know if we jumped through the windows or opened the door. As we were making our way back, the other team member had the vehicle started, taking his eyes off the creature. Me being so freaked out, I position myself correctly in the vehicle and start asking him questions. He stated that it was about seven to seven and a half feet tall with reddish brown hair coloration and skin, on two legs, and was going from one tree to the next as it made its way closer to us. With him starting the car, obviously, he had to take his eyes off the creature, and after being in the car asking the questions, we calmed down a little but were still very amped up, our adrenaline flowing. With the windows being down, we noticed the eerie quietness of the woods. We got the heck out of there. As you read this, and if you are a field researcher, you are probably thinking that there could have been footprints, seeing that the conditions of the mud were prime for them. I'd have to agree with you, but being so scared and young at the time, we were not going back to look.

As years go by and time has gone on, I have made a lot of friends in the Bigfoot community, and this brother in research did some research in this same area and talked with some of the local people who live in that area, and a few of them related to him that there's at least two of the creatures—a big, black male and a female that's around seven to seven and a half feet tall and reddish brown.

Since the very first incident in 2001, we had two other encounters where they walked towards us as well. One was during the daytime but never came close enough to where we could see it, but we definitely heard the bipedal footprints. And once, in 2009, we were researching in an area where we had had a rock thrown at us a few miles away. There were four of us this time, and we were walking on this dirt road. We spent about forty-five minutes on this dirt road doing vocalizations and wood knocking. We heard some stuff in the very far distance, but when we first pulled up, there was a dog that was barking and did not stop barking while we were on the road. We decided to turn around and head back towards the car, thinking nothing would happen because of this dog barking. While we were on our way, I asked an ex-team member to do a couple of wood knocks before we hop in the car and take off. So he did two wood knocks, and when he was done, we heard the heavy bipedal footsteps walking towards us from the woods on the dirt road. There were four of us at this time, and one of the ex-team member's wife was so freaked out that she turned on a 3 million-candle power spotlight and tried to see what was coming out of the woods. When she did that, the creature stopped, and we could not see anything coming from the woods towards us. We were all very spooked and standing shoulder to shoulder really close, just kind of frozen, waiting to hear any kind of movement, but nothing happened. At this time, we did not have a thermal imaging camera, but if we did, we would have picked up a heat signature. We did not enter into the woods and thought it would be best to leave the area to give the creature its space and respect.

Fast forward to 2018. This time, we are working with the town of Remer, Minnesota, and had been for a few years and still are. We go up and set up a table with some Bigfoot items and some merchandise. We also offer guided Bigfoot tours into the surrounding area where there has been Bigfoot activity, and this was probably the first year that we offered it, and we took two families of four out, and one of the families had to leave early, so that left us with the other family. We were out in the woods for about an hour and a half to two hours. When we do this, we equip the participants with parabolic dishes to help amplify sounds. And we try to elicit a response by doing vocalizations and wood knocks. In doing so, a nineteen-year-old woman was wearing the parabolic dish and was hearing what she described as grumbling or mumbling communication, but she could not distinguish what was being said, but it was a form of communication. This really touched her to the point where it brought tears to her eyes, because this is something that is not supposed to exist. And that happened to her, and still to this day, it gives me goosebumps relaying her story.

Last year, July of 2023, again we took people out on a guided tour, and in this exact same area a participant and an ex-team member had a sighting of a darker creature. We are continuing to research this area because it has been very eventful.

MQ: What is it that motivates you in your search for Bigfoot, and do you have an end goal in mind?

AD: What motivates me in Bigfoot research is to hopefully help to protect, preserve, and conserve the species. I hope to get some kind of law established so they are protected and where they live will be protected and not be destroyed or deforested. And I hope they will be recognized. I believe we are talking about some kind of homo species. And I say that based on the evidence that are in the footprints that are found. If we take a look at those casts, all of those look very human in form and not formed like a great ape with a divergent big toe going off to the left or to the right like we homo sapiens have on our hands that we call thumbs. So, I am under the impression that they are along the homo genus. Some people say that they do not need protection, but I disagree for the simple fact that the government and the timber industry are causing a lot of destruction to their homes and the woods that they live in, not to mention that there have been reports of them being shot. We have no idea how many there are or their population here in the United States, and with all of the land that is being taken for development, I believe it is very important to protect—where they go and where they are and their travel routes. But first we have to get more evidence that they are real to bring to the public, and the only way to do that is to get good video evidence, and unfortunately, a body is going to be needed as well. Seeing that we are a no-kill team, we could only keep our fingers crossed that we will come across a dead specimen while we are out researching and can document what we come across and take a piece of that specimen to bring back to science. And even after they are recognized as a living and dangerous species, and all the laws have been passed, my hopes are to continue researching them, because that would just be the tip of the iceberg. After all of that is established, then we have to move on to things such as their culture and how they teach one another as a parent would teach their children, and how their way of living is. How they talk, their language, how they hunt, the meanings of the different number of wood knocks, their strengths. There is just much more that we could learn, like, do their bodies fight off cancers and illnesses? And if so, how? How fast can they run on two legs or on all fours? We have all these questions, but they will never get answers unless we get them protection and recognized as a species, and that is one of the things that adds fuel to my fire and also to the rest of the Minnesota Bigfoot Research Team.

MQ: With all your experience, what is your opinion on whether Bigfoot is strictly a flesh and blood animal or if there might be some kind of paranormal element involved?

AD: When it comes to Bigfoot being flesh and blood or it having some kind of paranormal element to it, I am on the strictly flesh and blood side of that. We have to take a look at all of the evidence out there that has already been brought to light as far as Bigfoot film, footprints and castings, fingerprints. We have to think with common sense, and scientifically. Let's ask ourselves if there is another man or woman or primate species that has the ability to go through portals, or travel through different dimensions, or turn invisible. And because of what we do know of homo sapiens, or of great apes or any other primates, we can say no, that they cannot do that. And because a sasquatch can hide very well or be very fast and also be very quiet, it does not mean that they can disappear or go through a portal or travel through different dimensions. All of that stuff comes from humans assuming that they can and using it as a write-off to what they can't understand or comprehend. As a researcher, I remain open-minded, because if I'm closed-minded, then I'm not conducting proper research. So I take all of that and put it on the back burner, so to speak. I think it is an injustice to the field of Bigfoot research when people are going out there and saying that they have these paranormal abilities when there is no factual evidence that they do. We already are laughed at and have a hard enough time trying to bring the subject to the public and having the public look at it as a reality, and then when some throw in that the sasquatch have the ability to go through dimensions or can turn invisible and can open a portal at will for escape or for faster travel, in my opinion, it is a huge setback and is one of the reasons why this subject is still laughed at.

MQ: You're always seen wearing a large cross, and you talk often of your strong Christian faith. What role does that faith play in your life in general and in your work in the Bigfoot field specifically?

AD: I am a Christian, and Jesus Christ is my lord and savior. What does this have to do with Bigfoot research?—one might ask. But for me, because I know where I am going to go after this life is over, it really kind of gives me that sense of not being afraid while in the field doing research, because I know that I'm not alone. There have definitely been some very scary moments where I will say a silent prayer and feel peace while others feel that we need to get the heck out of there. My faith plays a huge role in my life. I try to be a humble man and to live by the golden rule, do unto others as you would have others do unto you. My faith has kept me very centered and balanced. No matter who you are, people are always going to talk about you or your research and judge you. But due to my faith, I take it all with a grain of salt. I do not sweat the small stuff, but instead, I move the team forward and let the talkers talk. Being a field researcher for 24 years, I have grown thick skin, and it no longer affects me as it once did. As it says in *Exodus 14:14*, "The Lord will fight for you; you need only to be still."

MQ: You started the first annual Minnesota Bigfoot Conference, now in its fourth year. How did that come about, and what do you think it's done for Minnesota and for the Bigfoot subject?

AD: I started the Minnesota Bigfoot Conference during the height of Covid-19, and it was held on August 8, 2020. I started it because I wanted the team to be able to give back to people in the Bigfoot community or locally here in Minnesota that may have an interest in Bigfoot. I myself have been to multiple conferences throughout the years and have made a lot of friends through attending them—friends that have become brothers and sisters in research, so to speak, have been on television, and some that have been researching for many, many years. The Minnesota Bigfoot Research Team wanted to get out the knowledge and the awareness that Bigfoot is here in Minnesota. We know that Minnesota has its fair share of Bigfoot sightings that have not been reported that some people have held on to throughout the years. Not only did we want to bring forth the awareness and education of Bigfoot, but we also want to be that safe platform along with Remer Bigfoot Festival for people to come to and share their sightings without being in fear of ridicule. The Minnesota Bigfoot Conference is all about education and awareness and being a platform for people to come and feel safe and to relay what they experienced, and I think we have done just that. Plus it also gives people a chance to see and meet Bigfoot researchers that have been on television or documentaries and get an opportunity to pick their brains and talk with them and even get a photo opportunity as well. This October 5, 2024, will be the fifth year of educating people, and we look forward to doing the Minnesota Bigfoot Conference for many years to come.

Another reason for the conference being in 2020 was because it marked the twentieth year since I started the Minnesota Bigfoot Research Team and thought it would be good not only to get the education and awareness, but to also have a celebration for this mile marker and for those who have been giving us ongoing love and support for the past twenty years through our videos to actually have an opportunity to come hang out and talk with us as well and meet the members of the team.

Besides getting the education and the awareness out there, it also gives people the opportunity to come to us and network with us about what they have happening on their private property that they would like us to come out and investigate, and it also gives us an opportunity to get more reports to follow up on as well, and to have that close-knitted relationship and trust with people. It also gives others a chance to, obviously, talk and communicate with others about their experiences as well. So I guess it is a multi-purpose platform for all to come and get educated and share and network. And this is something that would not happen if we did not have sponsorship, and we thank the area sponsors from Remer that have been with us since the very beginning, such as the Remer Motel and Campground, Bigfoot Gas and Gifts, and the Woodsman Café. They have been with us from the very beginning and believe in what we are doing and accomplishing by holding the MBC.

People can find us at *MNBRT.com*, the *Minnesota Bigfoot Research Team* Facebook page, *Minnesota Bigfoot Conference* Facebook page, *Minnesota Bigfoot Research Team TV* Facebook page, and on YouTube, and my personal page, *Elusive1 MNBRT* Facebook page.

Besides the Minnesota Bigfoot Conference being a platform for education and awareness, we also wanted to be a family fun activity as well, because we find that having fun while learning will help people hold on to that education a little bit longer. And plus, we want people to have a great time associated with the conference so that they will keep coming back for years to come and become regulars where we can know them by name. We have fun activities such as Bigfoot calling contests for adults and children with prizes awarded to the winners. We also have vendors with merchandise and a raffle as well. It's truly educational family fun for everyone in a safe environment. If you have never experienced the Minnesota Bigfoot Conference, I would like to urge you to attend.

MICHAEL HEXUM

Mike Hexum is a restaurant manager, hunting guide, and taxidermist who hails from Nashwauk, Minnesota in Itasca County, a rugged wilderness area near the Superior National Forest. Being in his sixties, he is the eldest member of MNBRT and affectionately known to the other members as Pops. He has had more than one Bigfoot sighting in his lifetime spent in the woods, the first one in his teens, and his experience is well respected. "They call me the Bigfoot man up here in northern Minnesota," he says. "I could talk about encounters and things Bigfoot related for hours."

Mike responded to questions for this book in December 2023:

MIKE QUAST: Can you describe how you first got interested in Bigfoot and how this eventually led to you joining the Minnesota Bigfoot Research Team?

MIKE HEXUM: I first got interested in Bigfoot back in the early seventies, having an experience off my deer stand where one walked out into a clearing and stared straight at me. It was about twenty feet away. I've been doing research for almost forty years up here in northern Minnesota. I met Abe back in 2015. I invited him up here because I was doing a film with *NPR News*. Shortly after that, I was invited to be a team member for the Minnesota Bigfoot Research Team.

MQ: Where have you found what you would call the best Bigfoot hotspots, and why so?

MH: Some of the best hot spots, I have found just north of where I live, up in northern Minnesota. There are two areas that go from east to west, which I called trackways. Along that area, I've had sightings, vocalizations, wood knocks, and even things thrown at me at night. People have asked me where the locations are. I usually don't give out that information because of ongoing investigations I do up here. I don't need people tramping around in the woods.

MQ: Are there certain techniques you use in interviewing witnesses and in conducting fieldwork?

MH: Interviewing a witness, I usually do first by phone, by talking to them I can usually determine whether it's an animal or their imagination. Secondly, if they prove credible, I'll talk to them in person. I can usually tell if they're telling me the truth by the movement of their eyes and body movements. I was told I would make a great police officer, but unfortunately about eighty percent of the time, I can determine what they have seen or heard as being an animal. I get a few reports on tree structures. I've actually went out and looked at them. Some of them are legit but most of them are wind damage from storms. You have to determine which is real and which is not, just like interviewing.

MQ: Can you recount some of your most memorable experiences in the search for Bigfoot?

MH: Most memorable experience number one, obviously, is the first one I seen back in the seventies. I've seen three of them in my whole career of doing field research. Second most memorable was up at the Nett Lake Indian Reservation; I was looking through the thermal imager, and this creature stood up and looked at me from about fifty yards away and then ducked back down and disappeared. I can't say it was a bigfoot—it most likely was a bear—but the vocalizations we heard that night—unbelievable. Unfortunately, none of our equipment was working right, so we could not get any recordings. Last but not least, we took all gas and no brakes out in the woods for the evening that night—was a complete shock and surprise. I had this young man by the name of Dylan with me, while Abe was twenty feet off the trail showing the film crew how to do wood knocks. This young man and myself were on the trail; this bigfoot walked out into the trail and stared at Dylan and I, started sidestepping side to side. That lasted for a few seconds, and then it walked back into the woods. This young man by the name of Dylan was completely freaked out, started running. I had to chase after him to catch him, but later that night walking out of the woods, we were being followed the whole way out. Very creepy.

MQ: What is it that motivates you in your search for Bigfoot, and do you have an end goal in mind?

MH: What motivates my search is, you never know what you'll find out in the woods. Artifacts dating back 200 years. I've seen animals that were known not to exist in Minnesota. Bigfoot is on the top of the list, of course. My goal is to keep doing field research. If I can prove beyond a shadow of a doubt that they exist, I would like to have a sanctuary set up for them in the woods where they can live.

MQ: With all your experience, what is your opinion on whether Bigfoot is strictly a flesh and blood animal or whether there might be some kind of paranormal element involved?

MH: In my opinion, based on some of the things I've seen, Bigfoot is a missing link. I believe they crossed the land bridge between Europe and the United States back during the ice age. Bigfoot is man that simply never evolved. I could see that in the face of the first one I seen at twenty feet away. It looked like a prehistoric man, all dark in color. Back in the middle seventies, there was a rumor that a hunter had shot a bigfoot just north of the Cook area. I had the opportunity to see it. It was in a glass coffin that was refrigerated. The smell was horrible. I could see a bone protruding through its finger. This creature was about five to six feet tall—not real heavy, in my opinion. Nothing could be faked to look as real as this did. It was later put on display. They called it the Minnesota Iceman. Later on, a fake was made and put on display. The one I seen, the original, was not a fake, in my opinion.

2

NORTHERN MINNESOTA BIGFOOT RESEARCH TEAM

The Chippewa National Forest is the smaller of two national forests in Minnesota, located in the central north and second to the vast Superior Forest that takes up much of the Arrowhead region in the northeast of the state. Both forests are rich in Bigfoot reports, though they are distinct from each other in that the Superior is more isolated and sparsely populated, while the Chippewa is much the opposite of that, with more surrounding towns and highways and visited by sportsmen of all kinds. The Leech Lake Indian Reservation inhabits the area, and Native lore about Bigfoot is very involved in the activity that takes place there.

Presiding over this hotly active area is a two-man team who call themselves the Northern Minnesota Bigfoot Research Team, made up of Bob Olson and Don Sherman. Both are now in their seventies but still very active, and they got into Bigfoot research late in their lives but have gone at it powerfully. Bob is an auto mechanic and owns his own body shop in the town of Deer River, while Don is a retired facilities manager for the Cass Lake Indian Services Hospital who now enjoys life as an artist through Sherman's Art and Design Studio and lives in the little town of Ball Club near the banks of the Mississippi River. As it happens, Bob is white, and Don is Native, which makes for a great combination in this mixed race area, so that any potential Bigfoot witness is going to feel comfortable in talking to one or the other of them. The collection of reports they have assembled is an impressive one, and their approach is fairly old school and low tech.

Bob and Don agreed to sit down with me to respond to a series of questions recorded on cassette tape at Bob's auto shop in Deer River on August 31, 2022.

MIKE QUAST: It's Sunday, August 31. This is Mike Quast, and I am with Bob Olson and Don Sherman at Bob's shop in Deer River, Minnesota, and I'm gonna run a list of questions by them here.

Can you recount how you first became interested in researching Bigfoot and how you first came to form the partnership that is the Northern Minnesota Bigfoot Research Team, and does your team have an ultimate goal?

BOB OLSON: Well, in 2006, my granddaughter—we were in the Cities, when we got back, my granddaughter left a message. She said, "Grandpa, call me!" 'cause she knows about Bigfoot. She said, "You gotta go up to Six Mile. There's Bigfoot tracks and all kinds of people up there." So I thought, all right, so I believed it, so I got some plaster ready and a bunch of stuff that I had, and I went up there and, sure enough, here were these deep footprints. I guess Cory Fraser, the grader operator, was grading and saw them. So that's how I got interested, and then when I cast a couple, then I heard about Don. He had been up there casting too. So we got together, and we started sharing stories and stuff, so that's when it started, as far as I know, in 2006.... And so, then a couple other people joined in. Jody Hansen from Keewatin was interested, and it kind of took off, but then, now we've kind of backed off. There hasn't been much going on, and we're getting older, and, you know, we're always on the lookout and listening for stories and stuff. But that's kind of what got me interested in it. And since then, I've cast about eight or nine different sets of prints in different locales. And one of the prints—a guy came in to look at my casts, and I showed him the one from Six Mile, and then I showed him the one some game warden's wife in Hungry Gulch forest in Walker was casting a print of on the side of the road. And a tourist stopped by, and he says, "What are you doing?" She said, "Well I'm casting a bigfoot print." He goes, "Yeah, right." "No, serious," she says, "there's creatures around here." So he started looking at it and saw the toes and stuff, and he started getting kind of serious.

Don Sherman (L) and Bob Olson (R)

He says, "I think I'll park my car and take a walk in the woods a little bit." About ten minutes later, he came out of the woods white as a sheet. He said, "There's more tracks back there." He says, "I'm getting the heck out of here." So, I had that casting, and compared to the Six Mile print, it's almost identical but a little smaller. The toe angle, the toe size, everything—so, that to me is confirmation. You know, five-toed Bigfoots are much the same. So that's what got me interested. That's where I'm at now. And a retired deputy sheriff, [name omitted], lives north of Deer River, and there's a gravel pit, and he lives probably a quarter mile from the gravel pit. He called me up. He said, "Go out in the gravel pit. Look for a house shingle, one of those tar paper shingles. He said, "I put it over a print. You won't believe it." Went over there and looked, and sure enough, under the shingle was a perfect print, which I cast. I started looking around. I cast another one, and then I cast one that stepped on a little hill that kind of went like this [demonstrates], you know. It's shaped like this because the foot slid, and I only got about a third of the big toe, but all the other toes are pretty good. So he's interested. He knows they're real. He's always on the hunt for stories and stuff. And [name omitted], who was a deputy sheriff and then quit—now he's running for sheriff again.... I was a reserve officer, and I'd ride with him at night— evenings, drive around. So we'd make a couple stops and stuff like that. He says, "I'm gonna show you something." So I said okay. So he drove all the way up to Togo. He's got the white sheriff's truck, drives down this just little bit of a clearing that maybe at one time was a logging road, and brush is scraping down the sides and stuff, and he goes back about a half a mile, and then it's all woods, and there's just a little bit of an opening up there where you could back up and come out. He stopped, turned like this [demonstrates], and about forty feet away is a birch tree. He shined his spotlight on it. He says, "See that tree?" I said, "Yeah." He said, well, he went up here two years ago, and he pulled back in here just to look around, and he says, "This is what I saw." Peeking out around the tree looking at him—Bigfoot, staring right at him. And he said, "That made a believer out of me." He said, "I just felt compelled to take you all the way up here and show you the tree." So I thought that was pretty cool when a deputy sheriff...

Another story I heard is, this boy worked at the Holiday—169 South Holiday—night shift. And he was on his way to work. He came off the—I think it's a split-end road, where it turns onto Highway 2, and as soon as he turned the corner, there was a bigfoot standing right in his lane in the highway. And it kind of stepped off and went into the ditch, and a highway patrolman pulls right up behind him. He says, "I'm kind of gun shy and paranoid. I thought maybe I did something I shouldn't have, you know." And he said, "I could see that deputy had his spotlight on it." It was only about seventy-five feet away, and the deputy's looking at it with the spotlight. And the lights are on, and it's lit up with the spotlight just like day, and he saw it. So he said, "I just left, and by the time I got to the Holiday, he was right behind me again with his lights on. I pulled into the Holiday to go to work. It was like 3:00 in the morning, and he whipped in there, and he said, 'Did you see that thing? Did you see that damn thing?'" He said, "Yeah, I saw it. What the hell?" And he neglected to get his badge number or car number, but there are five highway patrolmen in this northern Minnesota area, and none of them are talking. I've talked to like four of the five, and they just look at me. He says, "That's the gospel truth. I thought he was after me, the cop, 'cause he followed me right into the station." ...So, you know, you never know when you're gonna see them, what's going on.

MQ: Don, did you want to talk about how you first got interested?

DON SHERMAN: Well, when I met Bob, when they casted that track over in Six Mile—that's how I got interested. Well, I had previously seen a bigfoot back when I was about in my late twenties or early thirties. I was out deer hunting over by the Nushka Lake area. I was on the right side of the road; we call it the Go To Lake Trail forestry road. I was walking on an old logging road early in the morning, about ten o'clock—beautiful day out—and come up this little hill, and I saw this reddish brown thing. I couldn't identify it at first. I was saying, "What the heck is that?" It was probably about sixty yards away. And it was reddish brown, long hair. I couldn't see any facial features or anything, so I was trying to figure out what the heck this thing was. Well, I know it ain't a moose, it ain't a bear, and I was thinking, I had my 30-30 lever action with me, because I carry that for protection, and as I was looking at it, trying to figure out what it was, I heard this loud tree knock to the right of me, and it sounded like it was only like twenty feet from me. That's how loud it was. *Boom!* So I turned and looked, and there was hardly any underbrush, and there was just swamp, so I could see a long ways. There was nothing there. I turned back, and that son of a gun was gone. Was it a bigfoot? I don't know. That's the only thing I can think of.

BO: Tell him about your experience in West Texas in that area with Biscardi.

DS: Oh, that area there. Well, we were casting tracks along the river, me and Don Monroe. He's another Bigfoot researcher. I don't know if he's still alive or not. Anyway, he and I got through casting some tracks along a small river—more like a large creek. But anyway, as we were letting the casting material in the tracks dry, we took a walk to see if we could find any more tracks. And I had my FLIR camera with me, and I had my Walker Game Ears on, so I said I heard something walking towards us across the river. So I told Don Monroe. I said, "Don, there's something coming towards us. Let's get up on higher ground." And I caught a thermal image of this thing walking in the woods. It was no pig. It was walking toward the road where the bridge was, and it crossed the road. We went and looked for tracks the next day. Couldn't find any. Yeah, that was an interesting place.

MQ: Okay, I had a question about that 2006 Cory Fraser track report. There was such a media spotlight over that. What do you think it was about that particular report that lit such a fire for people and really put the area on the Bigfoot map when it wasn't the first such incident to take place there?

BO: 'Cause it was a trackway of prints on the right side of the road probably—what do you think, about 150 feet long? Hundred feet?

DS: Talking Cory Fraser? Yeah.

BO: And some of them were that deep [demonstrates], and he had graded the road, and it was a berm, and it had rained, so the berm was fairly soft, and for some weird reason, the left foot was in the road and the right foot was in the berm, like he was having fun walking on the berm. And the prints were about that deep [demonstrates], a lot of them. And they were absolutely so perfect, you could see the toes, and, I mean, there was no doubt. That's what made it such a believable thing. It was just track after track like that.

DS: And the toes also varied in depth. They were not all the same. They were varied.

BO: Yeah, each print maybe was a little different. And then one print—you could see right in the middle of the footprint was like a little stone, and it had stepped in it, and the print had actually stayed higher where the stone was, so you can't make that up. You know, it was obvious it was a bigfoot. They've been seen in that area a lot.

DS: That's the area I scout out a lot too, and, you know, I got a four-wheeler, so there's a lot of places we can go, and it can go through a lot of stuff and check out these areas where no man hardly ever goes.

BO: Did you hear about those two Native guys that were in the same area where Cory Fraser saw the tracks? They were driving along, and they rounded the corner, and there was a bigfoot standing right in the middle of the road, and by the time they stopped, they were like twenty feet from it. It was just looking at them in the car. So they actually said they drove around him and looked at him, and they went right back to the Bena store and went in there and blurted out their story to the guy working in the Bena store there. Yeah, they said, "You wouldn't believe it. We had to drive around him!" That's pretty good. So that shook them up.

MQ: Is there something about this area that you think makes it a particularly good habitat for Bigfoot?

BO: Absolutely. Endless swamps, high spots back through swamps where they could hang out, lots of food—they eat, what, cedar buds and who knows?

DS: Yeah, who knows. I don't know. Omnivores eat anything, like humans.

BO: Yeah, but it's just endless nothing for miles up in that area.

DS: It's a swamp—lotta swamp where nobody goes, and nobody bothers them.

BO: Yeah, you can't even get back in there unless you— I don't know how you could even get back to some of these spots, and that's where they are.

MQ: How do you go about investigating reports when you hear about them, and do the two of you have any differences in your style as investigators?

BO: Go look.

DS: Yeah, we're both— It's a learning thing. We're still learning Bigfoot researchers, learning about stuff like this here, and we're no experts. If there's somebody that tells you they're an expert, I believe they're not telling you the truth.

BO: Some old Native guy with a real heavy Native accent— I was talking to him about Bigfoot. I'm gonna talk just like he did. He says, "I'll tell you about the one that you see. He's the daywalker." I says, "Well, what do you mean?" He says, "He's the one that goes during the day and finds out where there's safe passage that night. And when it's dark, then they move all around all the time, but he's the scout, and we call him the daywalker." So I thought that was pretty cool.

DS: They're not just night activity—they're seen all hours of the day. I've gotten calls from people seeing them when the weather's like ninety degrees out. This lady called me up—she was coming from Red Lake up there—and she said it was about 1:00. She was just turned onto Highway 1 there where it tees, and she saw this thing standing on the road. She thought it was a guy in an overcoat. She thought, "What's a guy doing in an overcoat when it's this hot out?" So the closer she got, she realized it was not that; it was a sasquatch crossing the road.

BO: The son of an old lady that lived in Nary, Minnesota—it's a little berg south of Bemidji—she had an old farmhouse. Her husband was long since deceased, but she had a cute little white farmhouse. Well, she could still drive, she was in her eighties. She drove to Bemidji for supplies or whatever, and her son got a call. "Come get me! And I'm never going in my house again. Sell all my stuff. Sell my house. I'm not gonna live where there's monsters!" And he came to her house. It was in the fall. There was an apple tree with nice apples on it in the yard. When she pulled into the driveway, there was a bigfoot sitting under the tree eating apples, and it stood up, looked at her, grabbed a couple apples, and walked off. She said, "I'm not gonna live in a state where there's monsters." He moved her to some other state, sold everything she had. Sold the house. She said, "I can't live with monsters." She didn't even know what a bigfoot was until she saw that.

DS: I've got an interesting story here. This happened, I think it'd be three years now, right after deer season. My niece stopped in, actually, and she told me this story. I says, "Well, why didn't you tell it to me right away when it happened?" She said, "Well, the cops told me not to say nothing." So I said, "Well, tell me the story." She said, well, her and her friend were headed to Ball Club, this is just south of Ball Club on what they call the Willow Beach road, and not very far from that Mississippi bridge. And she said they were driving along; there was a car coming from the north headed south, and they were headed north, and she saw this thing come out of the ditch from the right side. And she said, "What is that? I don't know. Looks like Chewbacca!" So they watched it, and she said it had glowing red eyes. Then that vehicle that was coming towards them hit this thing. She saw it fly up, hit the windshield, go off into the ditch. So then it gets up and takes off, and it was headed towards the Mississippi River. It was just a little ways from there, about a block away. And so, she said they walked over to see if everybody was all right, and she said they were trying to figure out what the heck that thing was. So then, they called 911. Their car was pretty well smashed but still drivable, but the windshield was pushed in. So they said that they pulled the windshield off, threw it off to the side. And then the cops came. First ones to show up, I think, were the highway patrol, then the DNR showed up, then more cops showed up with dogs, K9s. Then they told my niece and the other people there what happened, so they described it to the cops. So then, they told them, "Well, you guys need to leave now." So they blocked the road off there for about four hours. So they left and headed back towards Ball Club, and then when I got wind of that story, I thought, well, that's kind of unbelievable. So I said, "Can you show me where this happened?" and she said, "Yeah, I've got an idea." So we went out and looked at the area where they hit it. So, I got to looking there, and I found the windshield. It was all busted up, and you could see the impact where the glass flew out in a fan pattern. So I picked up the glass, and I still got it.

BO: Any hair in it?

DS: I haven't even checked it. It's still in a bag. You know, what's-his-name wanted it. Cliff Barackman. Anyway, so that's the story on that there, and I published that story on Facebook on a sasquatch site, and some cop chimed in and said, "Oh, I got the police report on that incident, and that was a moose." He said they gave the meat to the local Natives around here. And I said that's a big lie right there. So I got a little ticked off about that, and I got off the site anyway."

BO: Some Native woman several years ago was driving. It was in the dark. She was driving down the West Bank road, and she sees all these cars and lights and everything going on and a couple helicopters, black helicopters with lights... and there's an officer stops her in the dirt road. She says, "What the heck's going on, is there a wreck or something?" He kind of stopped, and he paused a little bit, and he leaned in the windshield, and he says, "There's been a Bigfoot sighting." They were looking for Bigfoot. And she had to turn around and go back out. They had it all blocked off. Two black unmarked helicopters with searchlights. So they know. Everybody—the military, the sheriff's office, the DNR, forestry. They all know about them, but they won't talk about them. Somehow, they've been told, you do not talk to them. And I believe there's a government-Bigfoot-UFO connection, and everybody's staying dead silent about all of it.

DS: And they're making documentaries about this now. Bigfoot-alien connection. Ever get a chance to watch that documentary?

MQ: I've seen several, yeah.

BO: But we've watched episodes of the *Skinwalker Ranch*. They've been seeing UFOs. They've been seen coming out of portals, and weird stuff. One lady—she had quite a long field, and she looked out one day in the evening, and walking along the woods line looking at her was this bigfoot walking next to the woods line carrying a big glowing white ball... So there's high strangeness going on everywhere.

MQ: I'm glad you mentioned that car accident, because I had a question written down about that. I'd seen you talking about it on YouTube. Do you remember the date that that happened?

DS: I don't recall right now the exact date when that happened. It was right after deer season.

BO: It was only a couple years, isn't it?

DS: About three years. And there was about six inches of snow on the ground when that happened.

MQ: Okay, and was it daytime, or night?

DS: Just right after dark. It was about 6:00 when it happened.

MQ: Okay. Next question I had was, has your Bigfoot research had any significant effect on your daily lives, such as in how each of you makes your living?

DS: I'm retired, so it doesn't affect me at all. In fact, I have more time.

BO: I'm just tired.

MQ: Okay, you don't think you've lost business or anything because you're the Bigfoot guy?

BO: No, here's what happened around this area. When I first saw these tracks— I'm really open. I'll say whatever I believe. If I've seen a UFO, I'll say, "I just saw a UFO." Oh, baloney. I say, well, if you believe it or not, I'm telling you the truth. And they know I'm a straight shooter around here... So, I started telling people about it. And I tell everybody. Guess what? And I show my tracks. And another person would say, "My sister said she saw one." And people started feeling comfortable talking about it. And then Don, you know. And so, pretty much half the area around here believes and now is taking it seriously, and I think it all started from Six Mile with Don and I.

DS: So, a lot of people call if they have a sighting or something. They'll call either him or I. So we get a lot of calls, but it's been pretty quiet lately.

BO: Yeah. And then after that, talking to a gentleman over in Remer—they made Remer the Bigfoot capital of Minnesota, had their goings on and everything, but that started after us. And tell them about the Remer thing, that Bigfoot in the night time? Maybe you could compare the—on the game camera, the creature that—

DS: Oh, what the heck was that? That's the one where—

BO: The old man and the two sons were back in there? Rice Lake.

DS: Yeah. So, I did a comparison where their video caught this bigfoot crossing there... So then, we went out to the site there, and I took a picture of where the camera was, and I had Bob walk in.—you had your big coat on—and this thing was bigger than Bob. You're about what, six-five? We did a side-by-side comparison with that same tree where that thing walked by.

BO: The same walk as the Patterson Bigfoot.

MQ: Okay, this area contains the Leech Lake Indian Reservation, which seems to exist in pretty good harmony with the many White sportsmen who flock to the area, but are there differences you've noted in how Whites and Native Americans view the Bigfoot subject here?

DS: A lot of the Native Americans around here really don't talk too much about— If they have a sighting or something, they'll tell you about it, but that's all. My experience— I've been trying to get information out of the people who have sightings or seen these things. They don't really want to talk about it.

BO: They're kind of afraid of them, and the elders have said, "Don't mess with them." One kid by the name of Radar— I don't know who he is, but he called me up. He said, "There's a Bigfoot structure out in the woods." And he says, "I don't wanna dare go near it," and the elder told him, "Don't go near it." And I asked him if he would show me that, which I never did go up there, but he says, "I'll get you within a couple hundred feet of it." He says, "I'm not gonna go near it." Because it's something— You know, people are scared.

DS: When they went to that Bigfoot nest, people were getting sick, the ones who went there. They got sick.

BO: There's a psychic something going on, protecting the area. And the elders say, "Don't mess with them, don't look them in the eye. You know, don't go there." So they'll tell you what they saw, but they don't wanna go into details.

DS: If there's a track or a sighting, they will—we— You know I'm an Ojibwe myself. They put out food offerings. And this is to— It's like a peace offering.

BO: Pacify them.

DS: Yeah, "leave us alone," pretty much.

BO: Well, that gal from Six Mile hung a hindquarter of a pig in the tree there, and when they were doing tobacco offerings and dance ceremonies, there were thousands of people showed up a lotta times throughout the summer. And she hung that hindquarter in the tree up fairly high, and the next day, it was gone, ripped right out of the tree. So did a bigfoot do it? Did a bear do it? Don't know.

MQ: The Sammy Cleveland sighting on July 5, 2016, at Six Mile Lake got a lot of attention. Could you recount your memories and opinions of that case and what you think made it so significant?

DS: I had a chance to talk to Sammy Cleveland right after, so him and I, we went and— He brought his canoe, so I jumped in with his canoe, and we followed about where that creature was walking on the shore in the water. So, I could actually see the path of where this thing— You could see where it kicked over logs, and you could see the tracks and stuff in the water. Then when we got to shore. He showed me where the track was. I said, "Wow, that's pretty awesome." We were looking at it. And he said there was only four tracks, but I got looking at it; there were small toes turned out. So I ended up casting that one. Tried to cast the other one, but it was in too much water. So I got one decent cast out of it.

BO: Yeah, this thing wouldn't let him come to shore. It just kept pace with him. He'd go up and down the shore in the canoe, and it would keep pace.

DS: Finally, he had to call his friend to help him out, so his friend came over with his car. There's a landing right there. He was honking his horn, flashing his headlights to scare this thing away so he could get to shore. Finally, it disappeared. That's when it went into the woods, when he started honking his horn and flashing his lights.

BO: Yeah, when his buddy did that— That's when it left, so he could pull his canoe in and get out of there.

DS: Yeah, it's pretty amazing. What's interesting about it is, we were... the "Finding Bigfoot" team. Sammy Cleveland tried to tell these guys that he saw a UFO—different colored lights right above where he saw the bigfoot—but they don't want to hear that neither.

BO: No, they don't wanna hear it. They've been told to shut up, don't talk about it.

MQ: That touches on my next question. You guys have been

featured on the popular TV shows *Monster Quest* and *Finding Bigfoot*.
What were those experiences like for you?

BO: Was *Monster Quest* the one where they hit the van?

DS: That was the one over in Staples, Minnesota. That was more
of a Dogman. It had a snout.

BO: Dogman, yeah. And it actually— When it got hit, it kind of
bounced off the side of the van and slammed its hand down on top of
the hood and actually put big finger dents in the hood. I put my hand
in that, and it was like this much bigger than my hand [demon-
strates]. You could actually see the dents from the fingers when it
bounced off the car. We walked through and did an investigation,
hopefully trying to see something, and we didn't see anything. We
had Gene Hagen, another gentleman, with us. He's interested too,
and he's an outdoorsman—rugged outdoorsman with his trench coat
and his machete and stuff. And kids said they shot at the thing, so we
actually located a tree, where there was a bullet wedged in the tree,
with the thought that maybe it passed through the creature and there
was DNA on it, so he chopped that chunk of log out, and they sent it
in, and had it analyzed, the bullet taken out, and it came back as
inconclusive.

DS: That documentary that they did, they didn't tell the whole
truth of what really happened. They didn't say it was a Dogman.
They said it was a bigfoot. So they left that most important information out of that documentary.

BO: Was it before or after they hit it? It was on the roof of their
house?

DS: After they hit it. They went back in the house and heard
something on top of their roof, so one of the boys went outside with
his gun, and he saw this Dogman standing on the roof looking at
him... So, anyway, this Dogman was on top, and there was a birch tree
overhanging the house a little bit, so this thing grabbed a branch,
swung himself off the house, hit the ground running, and he could
hear the footsteps going away from the house, and about a minute or
two later, there was two of them howling back in their woods back
behind their house. So that's where Bob and I went the next day. We

went walking the woods behind there, but it was pretty thick back in there.

BO: Oh, mosquitoes were just terrible. I walked behind Don, and his whole back was black with millions of them on the back of his shirt. We were swinging with branches, getting them off us. It was a hot, humid day. But man, that was something. That was fun.

MQ: I was curious if there was a difference in how you were treated by the crews and the producers of *Monster Quest* and *Finding Bigfoot*.

BO: Much the same. You know, I think a lot of it is for show. You know, they want to make a show out of it. But a lot of it's based on fact, and pretty much, I believe all of the producers and stuff were believers.

DS: Except for the UFO incidents.

BO: Yeah, they don't like to hear about the UFO connection for some reason. And I believe that the government and sheriff's offices and stuff don't talk about it— I don't know, but there's some big coverup going on. Some big silencing thing going on.

MQ: Well, that pretty much touches on a question I had here towards the end. Where does each of you stand on the debate on whether Bigfoot is a flesh and blood animal or a paranormal creature of some kind; and if flesh and blood, do you think they're more humanlike or more apelike?

BO: I believe they're paranormal. I believe they can manifest into flesh and blood creatures that could maybe be killed. They leave evidence. They leave blood, hair, footprints... What was the other question?

MQ: When they're in their flesh and blood form, do you think they're more humanlike or more apelike?

BO: More humanlike. People say they can't shoot them because the face is humanlike. They don't look like an ape in the face. They look more human.

DS: A lot of the research— You know I do research online and stuff like that and hear other people's stories. When they see them up close, if you shave one of these things, they would look human.

BO: Might look like a, you know, rugged big-nose type, but very humanlike. You shave a bigfoot and put him in a nice set of clothes and have him walking down the street, and nobody'd look twice. Yeah.

DS: I'm gonna share a story here, and I don't know if I should or not unless I get his permission. I'm not gonna say his name. He tried to get ahold of me last year. He was having an incident out in his cabin out north of here, and he was playing around with this four-wheeler machine. He was trying to get it running good. It wasn't running good.... He said he got a little ticked off on it, so he jumps on his machine and guns it to see if he can burn the carbon out or whatever, and he didn't get more than twenty yards. He saw this thing out of the corner of his eye come out in front of him. And he couldn't stop. This thing grabbed the handlebar of his machine, and he got face to face with this thing, so he got a good view of what it looks like. More human that anything.... He described it as a boxer-face kind of nose. And grabbed his handlebar. When he hit the thing, it skidded the Bigfoot back a little bit. It slid back as he grabbed it. Next thing you know, last thing he remembered, he said he was flying over the air. This thing grabbed his machine, flipped him, threw him. And he said when he came to, his machine was upside-down. He was lying there on the ground, stunned, and his wife was coming running over and said, "What happened?" And he ended up telling her what just happened there. Yeah, that's about as close as you can get there. So I sent him a lot of pictures, 'cause I wanted him to sketch what he saw, and there was actually a lot of Bigfoot images—faces of what people think that they look like—so I sent him the link, and he went all through those faces, and he come up with one. He said, "This is what it looked like." *Finding Bigfoot* came out to visit him, but he didn't want nothing to do with them. They wanted him to sign something. He said, "I'm not signing nothing." He was a former police officer.

BO: They wanted me to sign too. I won't sign anything.

DS: Yeah. So that's a pretty interesting story there. That happened last year, about in July. I think it was last year.

MQ: Well, my last question was just to ask if there's any other special memories of searching for Bigfoot and researching their stories in this area that you'd like to share.

BO: How about the story in Hungry Gulch, when the people were going back in there, and the UFO tracks and the Bigfoot tracks under the UFO?

DS: Oh, yeah.

BO: There's a story for you—UFO-Bigfoot connection.

DS: I was in a Home Depot, and there was a lady I recognized, and she was walking towards me. "Hey!" She was waving at me. "Don, I got a story to tell you." So she said, "I was at the Hungry Gulch area. We were out four-wheeling," she said. And it was getting dark, and they were headed towards their car, and they saw this light back in the woods. So she said, "Dang, who in the heck built a house back in here?" She was a little ticked off about it. She said, "Let's go check it out." So they get over there, and it was a triangular shaped UFO on the ground. So they didn't get too close. So, they watched it, then it started rising up. So that's when they got scared. They head back to their ATV, jump on it and start heading back to their vehicle, and they seen this at treetop level then, and all of a sudden, she said it shot off. She said when it took off, it sounded like a freight train. So, anyway, as they were heading back towards their vehicle, they saw this jogger or hiker. They stopped and talked to him and said, "Did you hear anything funny?" and he said, "Yeah, I heard something here a little bit ago. It sounded like a train." So, anyway, they told him what happened. Anyway, they wanted to get back there the next day, but they couldn't, so they got back there a week later to that landing site—the UFO where it was on the ground—and there were Bigfoot tracks everywhere around it. I didn't get a chance. They didn't tell me soon enough, so I couldn't get out there. I never did make it. Yeah, that was a pretty interesting story.

BO: My beliefs on the sasquatch... I don't know how many people or researchers believe the things I do about it. I believe it's other-worldly. I believe it's from another dimension, and it can manifest and disappear at will. In my mind, it's debatable whether it could be shot, I've heard stories of it being shot point-blank, and it walks away like bullets have no effect. I believe there's a UFO connection. I believe they're definitely connected to alien beings. They've been seen in UFOs, on the ground under UFOs. They've been seen stepping out of portals. So there's a high strangeness to them, and I don't know if one will ever be shot or ever captured, for that very reason. One gentleman was out on a lake, and it was in the evening. The sun had gone down, and he said— He kept looking at a birch tree on the side of the road, on the shore. And he said, "All of a sudden, I see this creature step out from behind the birch tree." He says, "Now, why I was focused on that birch tree, I don't know, but I was." And he says, "It stepped back in behind the birch tree, and just a pair of red eyes came out, hanging in the air looking at me." And he said, "I got the hell outta there." Like, it went into the other dimension but just left its red eyes in our dimension to look at. And he says, "That's the truth. I swear it. I can't make it work mentally, but I know what I saw." So, these things are very strange.

DS: Yeah, there's a lot of stories where they've shot 'em though. There was a guy from Canada that shot one. He thought he was shooting at a moose. He came up on to it, and it was a bigfoot. He got a good view of it, but he didn't want to— I can't remember the name of the guy who shot it, but it happened quite a few years ago. But he got to examine the body really good, and he said it was more human than anything, just big and hairy. But he didn't tell anybody about that till, I think, about thirty, fifty years later. Because he was afraid he might get charged with manslaughter or whatever. Murder. 'Cause this thing looked too human.

BO: I go to River Lake Church. It's a Pentecostal church in Grand Rapids, and there's a gentleman that sells firewood. He's an older guy, and he knew I was a Bigfooter, and he told me a story, and when he started to tell me, he started shaking, because it was bringing the memory back. It was like twenty or thirty years before. He said they were down by Staples, and he said, "We were driving in the guy's pickup. I was a passenger, and we could see way up they had a stop sign. And he started to slow down, and I looked in the ditch to the right, and there's this black something, and I immediately thought it was like a tarp over some electrical thing, like maybe the telephone company, how they do their thing." And he says he realized that it was something like a creature, and he says, "By the time I told my buddy and got his attention, we stopped directly across from it, and it was like twenty feet in the ditch." And he said when he looked at it, it was about eight feet tall, and there was about a five-foot tall one in front of it—right in front, like an adolescent. And he said this thing looked at him with an angry look and took one step like this [demonstrates]—took his left hand and swept the little one aside, took one step, and brought his hand down on the roof of the truck and smashed it down about eight inches. Hit it right smack down on the roof. And the guy's just shaking. He says, "Just *boom!*" And he said, "We gotta get the hell outta there, and that's the god's truth," and he's just shaking when he tells the story. He said it just swept the one to the side so it could just—*pow!*—right on the roof of the pickup. The guy is a believable guy, and I don't know why he'd lie. But you hear these stories.

DS: I was in a coffee shop in Bemidji, and I was looking up Bigfoot stories. They have computers, so you can go and use them for free. Well, anyway, there was a lady sitting next to me, and she must have been watching me... 'cause she said, "Hey, I saw one of those." Something like that she said.

[Pause to turn cassette over in recorder.]

Okay, so she saw it, and then as she was driving along, she saw this bright—like somebody welding in the woods. And so, she drove a little bit further, and she saw these two hairy creatures in the ditch. She described that they looked like Ewoks—faces like an Ewok, you know? But their legs were turned backwards, for their knee. And, yeah, she watched those things. She said she was too scared to stop 'cause she was driving by herself. But yeah, they looked like Ewoks with their legs backwards.

BO: These Natives were working on a highway up in Boy River... and there was, I think, five or six of them. And one guy pointed. He says, "Look there!" And probably, I'm guessing, a quarter mile away, there's a bigfoot leaned up against a birch tree with its arms folded, watching them. And when they all turned to look at it—

DS: They heard tree knockings.

BO: Yeah, first. And then they looked, and it was standing up against the tree looking at them, and when they all looked at it, it dropped its hands and walked off. You hear that story?

DS: Yeah, they're supposed to have a photograph of it. I did see the picture, but it was pretty blurry. You couldn't make anything out of it.

BO: But they claim that's true too. We've got story after story after story of people seeing stuff. Hundred reports anyway, we've got documented. It seems like if you talk to somebody that believes in Bigfoot, they know somebody that has seen one, or, like, my brother's cousin saw one, or, you know, a lot of people know somebody that seen something. So that's pretty impressive.

DS: Yeah. I got a call one time. Somebody saw some tracks in Inger—on one of the side roads that goes toward Inger—so they put out plates of food for it. So, I went out to do some research and check out the area, so I seen where the old track was. It wasn't really worth casting. But me and my brother went to check out the area, and he was walking to the south of me, and I was— I found some tracks in the moss, so as I was checking these tracks, I saw this big spruce tree. I heard a loud *crash*, and this tree was shaking violently. I said, "What the heck?" So I hollered for my brother. "Dave, where you at?" He said, "I'm over here!" And he was on the opposite side, so whatever— The only thing I can think of—it had to have been a sasquatch shaking that tree.

The interview was winding down, and the phone then rang in Bob's shop, so we ended it. I was happy and appreciative for all the stories the two men had given me, and I am glad that they are in place in that Bigfoot hotspot for any further activity that might occur.

3

THE SHE-SQUATCHERS

A group of ladies with the quirky name of the She-Squatchers are an all-female team of Bigfoot researchers who have become a powerful presence in the Minnesota scene. Though there might be a novelty ascribed to them, they are not actually the very first team of their kind nationwide, but they are the first all-female Bigfooting team in the Midwest. I first learned of them in 2016, when they were in their early days and had traveled to a farm and home show type of exposition in the town of Thief River Falls, where they were holding one of their "Bigfoot Banters," in which they interact with the public and invite people to share their Bigfoot stories. There were just over a half dozen members of the team at that time from around Minnesota, but when I approached them after their presentation, the one who sat down with me and gave me her time was their founder and leader, Jen Kruse. She was engaging and fascinating, and we had a long conversation that day that would give me much to think about and lead to my beliefs about the Bigfoot phenomenon evolving.

There was a bit of a shakeup for the She-Squatchers after some time as they found that their roster of members was not quite the right mix, and a split in the group led to downsizing. Today, they are a group of just three tight friends, with Jen Kruse the leader and the other two being Jena Grover and Tammy Treichel, all in their early fifties. Until recently, Jen and Jena both lived in the Fargo, North Dakota-Moorhead, Minnesota area, where I also reside, but now Jena has moved down to Texas, where she has family. Tammy used to live in the region as well, and although she now lives far away in Virginia, she and Jena travel back to join Jen semi-regularly for various projects.

The Shes are a prolific group, with a dynamic online presence, including a website and podcasts. They also regularly travel all around the country—not just focusing on Minnesota, but attending expeditions and filming documentaries in other areas as well. I hope they produce a book someday telling their story, but so far, their forays into literature have been to partner with filmmaker Jason Kenzie in producing the 2022 children's book, *Adventures of Lil' Jay Jay: The Quest to Save Bigfoot,* and the 2024 comic book, *Searching for Sasquatch: The Hidden Treasure of Bigfoot Valley,* in which they are portrayed as whimsical versions of themselves.

I've been blessed to become friends with this trio of charming ladies, and in 2022, when I introduced Jen to Randy Bauer—the subject of my 2021 book, *Sasquatch Central,* who has experienced

Bigfoot activity at his property near Blackduck, Minnesota, since 2013 —it began a whole new chapter in which I've been able to go squatching with the She-Squatchers.

Also, I should mention that all three happen to be psychic, and that they bring this powerful tool to the search for Bigfoot.

In August 2023, while on a campout and documentary shoot by Jason Kenzie at Randy's place, the She-Squatchers did a recorded interview with me that started out with the fact that prominent paranormal researcher and cryptozoologist Loren Coleman from Maine had been instrumental in how the group first formed.

(Some equipment failure resulted in a couple of questions having to be redone later through online messaging, so this transcript is an amalgamation.)]

MIKE QUAST: Okay, so it's Friday, August 11, 2023, and I'm talking with the She-Squatchers, Jen Kruse, Jena Grover, and Tammy Treichel, and we are at Randy Bauer's place while on a Bigfoot expedition here, and they're going to be responding to a few questions. Can you describe how the She-Squatchers first came into being? I know it had to do with Loren Coleman. Whoever wants to start...

JEN KRUSE: So, in 2015, I did a radio interview with Loren for my radio show. I did not know anything about Bigfoot. I'd maybe seen partial—a handful of shows of *Finding Bigfoot* on TV. I did not know of Bigfoot at the time, but I wanted to do the interview, and he agreed to sit down with me at the ParaCon. At that time, he was educating me on the fact that there are bigfoots in Minnesota, and I didn't believe that. I grew up in the woods in Minnesota over by the White Earth reservation, and I was always in the woods, and I never saw or encountered anything that would make me believe that there were such a thing as Bigfoot. I had never actually spent any time thinking about whether there was a bigfoot or not; I just always assumed there wasn't. But he assured me that there were indeed bigfoots—Bigfoot was real, and he was in my home state of Minnesota—and he had an idea of sending women into the woods without men, dogs, or guns. He thought that would be a recipe for success in finding or getting closer or interacting with Bigfoot. He felt that the majority of these sightings of Bigfoot that are by roadways or where humans are—he felt that a lot of those are younger males that are probably out doing the things they're not supposed to be doing, and he felt these younger male bigfoots would be more likely to come in closer and look at some ladies who were less threatening without men, dogs, or guns around. So, I liked his idea. He kind of challenged and dared me to do it. He really wanted some ladies to do this. So, I jokingly volunteered, but by the end of the show, I legitimately volunteered to go out and give it a try. So, I did.

At that time, I grabbed some paranormal investigators that I knew, because they have night vision cameras that I thought we would need to be in the woods at night. So, our first time out was to a place called Six Mile Lake in Minnesota, and there had been a sighting there. We had been looking around there, and it was by a boat launch, but where we were at, from what we could see on the map, didn't seem like the place where that happened at. So we're driving around this lake... [partly inaudible but seemingly describes them going to another location] ...and I'm an energy worker. I feel energy on a physical level, sensations in my body, and I was literally asking to see and feel the energy of Bigfoot. When we got to the location, I felt this vibration that was new to me, so we went out and looked around, and we didn't see anything there that made me think that there would be Bigfoot there, but I really felt that this place felt different, so we threw down GPS coordinates and decided to come back to there.

And so, when we did, at that time, there were five of us on that first night, and we had an encounter there. You know, everybody got out of the car, and they went to the back hatch to get their stuff, and I already had my stuff, and one of the girls had handed me a FLIR—a cheapy FLIR thermal camera that she had borrowed from somebody else. She didn't even know how to work it. She just knew you would pull the trigger, and it would take a picture. It didn't even have an SD card in it. She didn't know that. But she handed it to me. What is it? And I had never played with a thermal before, and I thought it was very cool, so I'm scoping out the woods and hoping to see a deer, a fox, a rabbit, anything, I wanted it to show up on it. So, I'm scoping out, and then I pointed out in front of the car, and just out by the trees, there was somebody standing there on the thermal. And I thought it was one of the girls that had walked up, and it was so dark I couldn't see out there, so I was like, "Who's out in front of the car?" Nobody answered, and I kept asking, "Who's out in front of the car?" And with my anxiety in my voice, because no one was answering. And then Marlowe, who was there that night—she recognized that I was nervous about something, so she ran up to the front, and she looked at this thing, and she saw what I was looking at, and so she looked up from the screen to see— She could see something there with her eyes, and she gasped. And she said, "Ah, I just saw eyes!" So I looked up to see if I could see eyes, and I didn't, but when I did that, I had moved the camera. And so, then I was trying to find it again, and it was gone.

And so, we decided to walk into the woods where that thing was standing just outside. So, a few of us started walking into the woods, and we didn't get very far in before rocks started coming through the treetops. We watched one fall three feet in front of us and bounce. And again, I didn't know anything about Bigfoot, so I was like, "Is that a rock?" And then here comes another one bouncing right next to it, and I was like, "Yeah, I think that is a rock." And I'm like, "Somebody's throwing rocks at us?" I didn't know that Bigfoot was known to do that, had no idea. And neither did any of them. We didn't know anything, nothing. And so I was just dumbfounded that something was throwing rocks at us. If you've ever been over there on that side of Six Mile Lake, it's just woods. Just woods and road, and mosquitos.

JENA GROVER: Mosquitos throw rocks at you over there.

[Riotous laughter from all]

MQ: I have been there, so I know.

JK: So, yeah, I was just like, "What is happening here?" And so, I really felt like, okay, whatever is throwing rocks doesn't want us to walk this way, so we backed up. And so, we're standing there, and we're like, "Okay, now what?" And so, one of the girls said, "Hey, maybe we should do one of those Bigfoot calls like they do on TV, and so she does a "whoop," and a much louder "whoop," and we just all stood there waiting to see if something whooped back. But we didn't get a whoop back. Instead, there was movement. And it wasn't from the left side of the road where the rocks were coming from. Instead, it was coming from the other side of the road. And so, something started walking toward us, and it was very obviously bipedal—very big, 'cause you could hear it stomp-stomp, and the sticks—everything was just cracking as it walked. And we all just turned toward the sound with our night vision cameras, and then we realized these cameras don't light up the forest like they do haunted houses that they usually use them for in their paranormal investigations, so they were pretty useless. We couldn't see what was making the sound as it was coming toward us. And then, it was as if somebody snapped their fingers, and that sound of something walking toward us multiplied, and now there was something coming toward us from multiple directions. And we all circled up, back to back, facing out, all straining to see what's coming, and none of us could see anything, and they were really scared. And it was kind of scary.

But then, when we all turned to do the tobacco thing—and so, we were on an Indian reservation, and I am part Ojibwe, and so I took tobacco in my hand, and I started to pray out loud in Ojibwe language. I did a very formal protocol greeting that I was taught that you do when you start naming relatives. You know, you're supposed to do that so they know who you are. And then I started thinking, [Ojibwe language], thank you to Bigfoot. And as soon as I said that, all of the sound and movement stopped. It just stopped. It didn't retreat; it stopped. Everything stopped, and it was just silent. And I was like, "Yeah!" I was all excited inside, because when I had talked to the elders from the tribe, and I had talked to elders from different reservations about Bigfoot, there was one particular elder from the Turtle Mountain reservation who told me that you can pray to the [Native name for Bigfoot] and ask him for help, and he will help, and so, when we pray to the Great Spirit, we say who we're trying to communicate with and then ask for help, and so I think when Bigfoot and the sounds stopped, to me, I just had a confirmation of what the elders had told me. And so, I was really excited, and I was just like adrenaline rush at that point, like, you know, that's confirmation for me.

Although, the girls that I was with that night—not these girls—had no idea what I had just said in the Ojibwe language. You know, they didn't know that it was right after I said thanks with Bigfoot. They were just, "Okay, let's get in the car. Let's go." And we got in the car and drove away. And as we're driving away, you know, the things they were saying were—I don't think I really want to find Bigfoot anymore, this is way scarier than Bigfoot flying off the wall. You know, this was way scarier than that. Maybe he could just cross the road in front of us—that would be okay. Things like that.

So, needless to say, I needed girls that were more fearless and had the commitment, and really doing this as a group has been quite the commitment. It takes drive to do this, with our own money, and just a function of time, time commitment. There's been a huge time commitment.

JENA GROVER: Agreed, very much so. But you know what? It's the best thing ever. It's opened a whole new life, I think, for all of us. I've seen things that I cannot believe I've seen.

JK: Well, as I got home from that weekend, I met up with Jena, and I was telling her what happened that weekend, and she was so mad at me for not bringing her with me the first time. But I was embarrassed to tell my friends that I was going to look for Bigfoot. I was embarrassed, because I didn't believe in Bigfoot, and here I was gonna go look for Bigfoot. And then I had an experience that made me go, "Okay, I think Bigfoot's real" and I wanna tell everybody, or at least my friends, so she was on board after that. And I also told Tammy, but things weren't working out. She couldn't join us right away, but she did as soon as she was able.

TAMMY TREICHEL: Consider all the traveling that we've got to do, places that we never would've traveled to that we've gotten to go and see and investigate and meet people, like Bob Gimlin.

JG: Well, the people alone that we've met just who are fans of the cryptid community are incredible. And they've all been so nice to us.

I mean, maybe not all, but we don't expect everyone to like us. You know, people have been amazing.

TT: It's been a great journey.

JG: Yeah, and it's gonna continue being a great journey. This is not where it ends.

TT: We're just getting warmed up.

JG: Yes. Yay!

MQ: That kind of leads into my next question. You are such an active and prolific group. Can you each describe your occupations and how you are able to spend as much time away doing all the appearances and expeditions that you do all around the country?

JK: All right. So, I'm a self-employed holistic healer. I have my own practice, and I just work really, really hard when I'm home and save up money for time off, because I don't have any time off. And you know, at first, when we were doing events, we were pretty much traveling on our own dime, and then now, we get help with travel expenses and all that when we're going to an event. We also get the opportunity to investigate all over the country from one coast to the next to the other, and that has been a blessing all within itself.

JG: In the beginning, I searched for a classy Bigfoot charm and couldn't find one I liked, so I worked with a local business to make a unique charm of my own. I had previously been making sea glass jewelry and decided to add Bigfoot into the mix. I sell jewelry at events, and a few other items. The money made helps fund a small portion of my travel cost for events and expeditions. I'm also blessed to have a small passive income as well. This helps me utilize my time for amazing adventures. I'm also blessed to have people in my life who emotionally support me and my travels, which is very important. My blessings and struggles balance these days. You can enjoy the blessings much more when you've lived through your worst pain. Life is so hard sometimes, but that's what makes it beautiful.

[Author's note: Jena is being very brief here when mentioning her worst pain and hard life. In other interviews, she has gone into detail about a medical crisis she had in 2009 in which her body became septic for forty-eight hours after a doctor accidentally nicked her colon during a routine laparoscopy, leading to emergency lifesaving efforts during which she had a fascinating near-death experience that ended with her being sent back from the afterlife feeling it was not her time to go and that she had more to do. Her NDE happened six months after her brother died and five years after her father died. Due to the repercussions of the event, she is unable to work at this time. She struggles with chronic pain, chronic nausea, post-surgical issues and scar tissue, unremovable recalled mesh, and Crohn's. She said she is working hard to heal her mind and body through food, exercise, and music. She doesn't let the struggle stop her. Jena has shared with me that she has created her own Bigfoot charm in her jewelry sold at events and is fortunate to own shares in her family's farm, which allows her to take some time to go adventuring with the She-Squatchers.]

TT: My profession is adventurer/explorer. My current position is working at a scuba dive and swim school. My job is very flexible, which allows me to pursue my passions. It helps that one of those passions is also scuba diving.

MQ: I normally ask researchers if they have any particular techniques they use in both fieldwork and in interviewing witnesses, but you have the unique quality of being psychic and of using the skill of remote viewing, so how would you respond to that question with that in mind?

JG: We have tried multiple techniques, and, in my opinion, remote viewing has been very reliable. Jen is our main remote viewer. Being psychic—I prefer using the term receiver of information—can be a major advantage in the field.

TT: Being psychic and a remote viewer gives me an advantage in researching and interviewing. While researching, I am able to remote view the area and find the best areas to have the opportunity to interact with Bigfoot and find evidence. While interviewing witnesses, I am able to visualize as the witness speaks, which I feel gives me a better connection with the witnesses and their interaction/sighting.

JK: [This answer is from online messaging.] This brings up the science of being psychic, and I think that it's very important for people to understand it better. Everyone has these abilities available to them, just waiting in their subconscious mind. Science tells us that the human brain works at 400 billion bytes per second. That's not a potential. That's what it's actually doing. Out of that 400 billion bytes, the average human is consciously aware of only two thousand bytes per second. That's almost nothing. I tried to make a pie chart representing this statistic, and it wouldn't even accept it, because it's much too small of a percentage to even show up as a single hair in a full circle pie chart. Why is that significant? We are sensing so much more than we are consciously aware of. Seeing, feeling, hearing, and knowing so many things. We all get these gut instincts that we eventually learn to trust in. Where do they come from? They come from these senses that remain in our subconscious awareness, but they squeak out to give us warnings sometimes. You know that guy who gives you the creeps but looks okay, hasn't said or done anything that makes you suspect anything... but still, your gut instincts are telling you to be cautious of this person. That's the subconscious trying to give you information. Another example: when we think of someone and then the phone rings with a call or text from them. How did we know? It's something we all know in our subconscious minds.

How does this apply to being psychic? We can all learn to tap into that extra knowing that we already have inside of us. Imagine looking at an eagle through binoculars. You can see the eagle really well, but that's about it. However, you can easily turn your head a bit and see what is also out there. That's kind of what it's like to begin accessing this extra information that's waiting for us in our subconscious minds.

As a psychic, I've used my abilities to help locate missing people, lost dogs, and now we use it for locating Bigfoot hotspots. As for using this sill set in looking for Bigfoot, we use what we call *geographic remote viewing*. It's different from the remote viewing that others talk about, which is called *controlled remote viewing* and was aided in being developed by our government agencies many years ago. In geographic remote viewing, we utilize satellite imagery to look at locations while asking questions such as "Is Bigfoot here? Is there any Bigfoot evidence we could collect here?" And so on. What we see on the satellite image changes in reaction to the question if there is something there. Others wouldn't see it. The picture doesn't actually change, but in our mind's eye, we begin to see a picture or a short movie in response to the question we asked.

I'm the primary remote viewer in our team. When I see something of interest, I drop a GPS pin next to it and then send the coordinates to my teammates, Jena and Tammy, asking them what they see at that general location. If they come back with the same things which I saw there, we call that a "good hit." If we are able to go there, we do. This is how we captured the thermal FLIR footage on the mountaintop in Tennessee, first did a remote view and found a location. My team confirmed it as a good hit, so we went up there and parked near the location of the GPS coordinates. It was so dark, we couldn't see anything. Before getting out of the car, I pulled out my phone once again and still had WiFi signal, so I asked if there were any Bigfoot here right now? I saw one just thirty feet from the car and pointed in its direction, telling my teammates there is one thirty feet that way. Tammy pulled out Jena's FLIR camera and pointed it that way, then she got very excited to see it there. She didn't know how to make the FLIR record, so she was pushing all the buttons while watching through the view finder. The Bigfoot raised its arm and reached over to scratch under its opposite elbow. She saw all the hairs hanging down from the arm. Jena finally aided Tammy by hitting the record button, and we captured eighteen minutes of footage of this Bigfoot.

Another example: we were going to look around the area of Twin Valley and Ulen, Minnesota, for a weekend. I did some remote viewing of some interesting areas and saw very clearly a bigfoot with a mountain lion, like they were together. I sent the coordinates to the team, asking what they saw in this general location. Tammy came right back saying, "I see a bigfoot with a mountain lion." That's a good hit; however, I have a healthy fear of mountain lions, so we only looked into that forest from the edge.

I'm not afraid to admit that I'm not as fearless as my teammates are.

In addition to remote viewing, we all have various psychic abilities which complement each other as we work together. I can see auras, the energy field around living things; however, it takes me a while and have to try hard to see them. Tammy sees them very quickly and easily. How could this be used in our search for Bigfoot? If something is hiding behind a tree, it's possible that Tammy could see its aura, which can often be quite large. I'm at work at the tribal college. When a client comes in, I'll stop messaging and pick it back up later.

We all have varying degrees of abilities in animal communication. I've practiced trying to telepathically communicate with the white-faced saki monkeys at our zoo in Fargo.

As an empath, we can feel what others feel, whether that be emotionally or physically. This is helpful when an animal is hiding and scared. I can often sense their fear and location.

Jena has been quite successful in predicting dangerous events. One example is, I had recently acquired a new night vision camera that I wanted to test out. I had planned an evening in the country where my Mom had been staying with a friend near Heiberg Park outside of Twin Valley, Minnesota. It's a river valley with woodlands surrounding it. Jena called to tell me the following: "The danger in the darkness is very real, Jen." She didn't know what that meant, but later that night, when the sun went down, I was outside with my mom, playing with the new night vision camera. It turned the dark night into the day. However, when I pointed it in one particular direction, suddenly it was all dark—couldn't see a thing. I kept turning, and the camera was working just fine, seeing into the darkness in other directions, remaining just dark when looking to the east. Suddenly, we heard something in that direction. It huffed at us. Then you could hear it breathing, and its movements, as it was running at us. I was still trying to see what it was through the night vision camera while my mom had taken off running to the building behind me. She yelled at me when she reached the doorway to get over there right now. Then, I remembered Jena's warning about the danger in the darkness being real. I turned and ran to the building, and we locked the door behind us. To this day, I don't know what charged us, but it sounded large and angry. I'm thankful for Jena's warning.

Jen then messaged the following assessments of herself and of each of her teammate's abilities:

TAMMY: Tracker, scuba diver, kickboxer, psychic medium.

- Sees auras/energy fields.
- Animal communicator.
- Sees entities with naked eye.
- Removes negative entities.
- Medical intuitive.

JENA: Tech advisor, hiker, singer, psychic medium.

- Predicts danger.
- Sees visions.
- Receives messages.
- Suspected alien abductee.
- Near-death experience.

JEN: Team leader, public speaker, psychic medium.

- Geographic remote viewer.
- Empath.
- Otherworldly communicator (water spirits, djinns, little people).
- Feels energy on physical level.

Jen then reiterated some of what she had stated earlier about human senses:

JK: The human eye can only see between 430–770 Hz. Our ears can only detect sound between 20 Hz–20 kHz. These ranges make up a fraction of the total sound and light frequency range. This means that there is a lot going on that we cannot see or hear.

MQ: Jen, as leader of the team, you place special emphasis on your Native American heritage and its perspective on the subject of Bigfoot. How do each of you feel about approaching the subject from the Native point of view?

JK: Well, I approach it from my Native point of view and my own rational mind in seeking to have more experiences. But I do. Especially when I'm on the reservation, I follow all the ceremonies, the formal greetings and traditions and customs that I was taught. And, you know, before going into the forest, I get tobacco. I give back something, and do all the things that I was taught. And I feel like it puts me in the right mindset and place in my heart and lets them know that I'm coming in a good way, which is what I was taught. And then, they don't have to do that with me, but they don't mind that I do that. They have their own beliefs that they follow that doesn't go against anything what I believe or follow. It all just works very well together.

JG: I feel like it's a beautiful addition to our team. I think her knowledge and their belief system as far as Bigfoot being or representing the most honest life— Or, what did you say, Jen, that they reflect honesty?

JK: Yes. In the seven pictograms in the teachings of the Ojibwe, each of the seven teachings is represented by a specific animal. Like, love is represented by the eagle. Humility is represented by the wolf. But honesty is represented by Bigfoot because he lives the most honest life, so, literally, his name in the Ojibwe language is *Gitche Sa'be*, which means "great honesty."

JG: And I also think, too, besides that, which is a beautiful thing, I also think that Ojibwe— Jen knows the language, and she's able to communicate. I think that throughout history, that they do know that language, and we have an extra benefit of her knowledge.

TT: The history of Native Americans with Bigfoot is that her ancestors lived side by side and worked with Bigfoot. So they speak the language, they know her ancestors, so I think that that gives us a closer connection with them.

JK: An ancestral connection.

MQ: Okay, this one you may have answered already, it's a standard question. Can you all just describe some of your most exciting and intriguing experiences you've had in the search for Bigfoot?

JG: Ah, I don't want to sound like a weirdo, but I mean...

JK: Yes, in May. You saw a bigfoot in May.

JG: Yes, we were here in May, and we were walking down the line of electrical poles, and Randy was talking to us, and he happened to, you know— I happened to be looking down, and I saw this something that looked almost like a tree stump next to the electrical pole, but it was really tall, and I thought, oh, well, Randy's not saying anything, so whatever. So we all kept walking, and then, he brought us to this electrical pole with hair that he said had been tested and been proven to be Bigfoot hair, and I was focusing my camera in on this hair. I wasn't really focused in on what they were saying, and all of a sudden, I hear Jen say she saw something. And I was like, "What?" And I started asking; I said, "Oh my gosh." I said "What side, what side?" And she said the left. What I had seen was on the right, and she goes, "Is it still there?" And I put my phone down, and I looked, and it was like [huge gasp], "No..." It was the really, really— you know, I want more. You know, I want specific. I want an eye connection. I want that beautiful connect.

TT: You want a face-to-face interaction up close and personal.

JG: Yeah. Yeah.

JK: So you know I saw the one on the left.

MQ: Yeah. Okay, what motivates you in your work in the Bigfoot field, and do you have an end goal in mind?

JK: Ah, okay, I say that this is what happens when your kids grow up and they go unsupervised. It's all their fault. ...Um, but you know, for me, it started out as a hobby and curiosity, and I've always been interested in mysterious things and learning about things that I didn't know about, exploring the great mysteries of the world. And for me, doing this is to satisfy my own curiosity. It's been never-ending, to be continued, a cliffhanger. When we go out looking, and we find something, it just leaves me wanting more. Found out something, but, I feel like okay we found something, but now I want to know more.

TT: Every time we have experiences, and we get closer and closer, it just makes us want more. And we want— You know, the end goal, I guess, for us would be personal interaction, face to face. You know, sit down and interact with them. We would never give away their location. We would never give away anything they didn't want us to give away, but we want the experience for ourselves. We want to interact with them on a level that nobody else has.

JG: Yes. And for me, you know, I've been so interested in spirit ever since I've been little, and you know, once you find out that ghosts are real and you don't need to really— I don't look to find the evidence of ghosts anymore, because I know they're there, and I can interact with them. So, after my NDE in 2009, I was changed. I was a new person, and I was really looking for something incredible. I wanted to do something with my life. I'd lost the feeling of worry that people were— You know, I just lost the fear that I held on so tightly to before I died. You know, so without that fear, finding out Jen had this team, and she was going out into the woods— I was looking for, you know, companionship. You know, I was looking for exercise, and I was looking for a sense of adventure. I wanted to start living. After dying, you want to live. And I was so excited to start it, and that's what fuels me. But since I've been on a team, I've seen things that I would never have thought would exist, and that just means there's only more to come.

TT: I want to do all the things. I want to go all the places, have all the experiences. Life is so short, and there's so much to see and do, and I just wanna do it all.

JG: We're only halfway there. We're halfway done. So we've got fifty more years to pursue everything.

JK: And I want to add to something Tammy said about— We would never tell their location. So if we found a Bigfoot village, we would not tell people where it is. We would not tell them where it is.

TT: We would not let them, you know, come in and steal things...

JK: I've had nightmares about that. I've had nightmares about that.

TT: We just want the experience. And we won't even care, you know, if anybody believes what we find.

JK: We want love, and learning, and relationships, and growing and learning.

TT: We just want to experience for ourselves. We don't care if anybody else believes us or not.

JK: I've been saying that from the beginning. We can't be detoured if somebody says, wow, they could've done that, or, you could've hoaxed that, or whatever. You just have to expect that that's how people are, and that's not our goal to convince anybody. Our goal is to satisfy our own curiosity and our own need for adventure and to share what we found along the way, and people can love it or leave it. It doesn't matter. And that's just our attitude about that. And in remote views, I will say that I have been remote viewing for other researchers in other parts of the country, and there have been times where I've seen Bigfoot, and they've put their finger up to their mouth, like to say, "Sh... Don't tell." And then I don't tell where they're at. And there was one specific one that I did recently for a team in Ohio that had a celebrity with them that night, and I knew the celebrity was more aggressive in his looking, like would chase after things in the forest or whatever, and I saw groups of them. And so, normally when I remote view for them, I actually give them locations of where they are and what they're like. Their ages, their demeanor, things like that. And I told them everything that I saw there, except for the younger group that went "Sh... Don't tell." I didn't tell that night. I knew they were going up that night, and so in the morning, I sent the one guy a message, and I said, "Oh, by the way, the thing I didn't tell you last night was, there were also some here, but they were younger, and they were telling me not to tell. And I totally understood that, because I feel like he would have run after them... So, there is that. Respect, don't tell.

MQ: Okay, with all your experience, what opinion does each of you have on whether Bigfoot is a natural flesh and blood animal or if there might be some kind of paranormal element involved? Are you all of one mind on this, or is it something that you debate?

TT: I will start. I think it's funny, because I think both of them are starting to come towards my point of view, but I always would preface anything— Any time I'd answer that question, my views are my own, and it doesn't mean that they believe what I believe. It's just my views. I believe that they're interdimensional beings. I believe that while they're on this plane, that they are physical, but I also believe that they are physical because they concentrate on being in this dimension, and I think that they are not from this dimension, and I think that the reason they can get away so quickly is that they have to concentrate to be here in the physical form on this plane. And if something breaks their concentration, if they get scared or startled and they stop concentrating, they disappear, because they can't be here without concentrating, because they're not from this dimension. So, I feel that they're interdimensional. I feel that they can be flesh and blood while they are on this plane, and that they can travel through dimensions, through portals. And, do I think that they are related or involved with the aliens? I think that they are probably... I think that what we believe is aliens is not really the way it is. And I think that aliens is strange to us. And that being, yes, high strangeness— They are all strange. They are not of this dimension. And, could they be aliens? In that sense, sure. Do I think that they are involved with the grays and things like that? I'm not sure. You know, there've been times where, you know, everybody says where there's UFOs there's Bigfoot, and where there's Bigfoot there's strange lights. So, I think there's a lot of things that we just don't have enough information about to make that decision, but, yes, I do believe that they're interdimensional and not just a flesh and blood creature.

JK: For me, you know, I spent a lot of time talking to the elders of the tribe and collecting information that they share, and I respect everything that they share with me and hold it sacred, and I just cherish it. But I have this rational part of my mind too that says, okay, I can understand what they're saying, but I need to experience that myself to really fully grasp it, because it's just hard for me to fully grasp that they can travel instantaneously, physically, from one place to another with thoughts through the ground, I mean, which is what they told me. And I was like, okay, I hear what you're saying. Are you talking about a portal? And they're like, yeah, and I'm like, okay, but still, that rational part of my mind needs to experience that, to see the evidence of that for myself.

So that's just the rational part of my mind. But have we seen things that point in that direction? Sometimes we have. You know, but at the same time, I do think they are flesh and blood. I feel like they have a deeper connection to the Mother Earth as a whole, and they're more aware of that natural connection amongst all living things. And humans can be aware of that connection. We're the only ones who fell out of harmony with nature. And I could list all kinds of scientific points on that. You know, Dr. Cleve Backster, in the sixties, was doing experiments with the philodendron plant and his lie detector test. You can watch it all on YouTube on *The Secret Life of Plants*, or *Panic in the Cabbages*. Just look them up on YouTube. You can see his experiments. And he was the CIA's guy for doing lie detector tests, but he started doing the tests on plants and animals, and he was realizing through these tests that plants can sense what others are going through, not even in the same room. And so, at the smallest level of measurement, life is sensing each other and is more aware of the inner connection with all things, and that's a natural state of being. And humans are starting to become more aware of that again, I think, and that's what people are calling empaths and, you know, when they stop calling it a curse and embrace it and allow what it really is supposed to be, it's a beautiful thing. Become more consciously aware of their inner connection and interdependence and interrelation with all things, with all that is. And that's a natural state of being that— I think Bigfoot lives in harmony with nature at all times like that. And just because we can't see something doesn't mean that it's not there. And when I say that I'm not saying anything woo-woo. I'm talking about the human brain in general. There's science behind this. The human brain thinks at 400 billion bytes per second. That's not a potential. That's what it's actually doing. And yet, the average human is only consciously aware of 2,000 bytes per second out of 400 billion that it's actually aware of. And so, all of that's going on in the subconscious mind, so we're seeing, hearing, physically feeling, sensing things in our subconscious mind that we're never even consciously aware of. That's where our gut feelings come from. That's where intuition comes from. A little bit of it leaks into the conscious mind and gives us those feelings. But if we could tap into a little bit more of that awareness we could—like looking through binoculars and looking at an eagle, you can turn your head a little bit and look at something else there, and that's as easy as it is to shift your conscious awareness to see and become more aware of what else is there. And so what I'm saying is, we are very, very consciously unaware of the things that are surrounding us. And so, when they say that sometimes people—one person can see a bigfoot and the other doesn't. It doesn't mean that it wasn't there. The other person could've seen it in their subconscious awareness, and it never entered into their conscious mind. I mean, there's so many scientific angles to that that nobody ever talks about. Does that make sense?

MQ: Uh-huh.

JK: Okay. Jena.

JG: You know, when I first joined the team, I thought it was a flesh and blood. In fact, I didn't even think they existed. I was a complete skeptic, and it was a very long time before I even believed that they could exist, and it took one experience for me to say "Okay, this is it. I believe now." And then, it was— What is it? I really believed it was flesh and blood this whole time. In my head, I was really, pretty, like eighty percent sure that it was flesh and blood. And it wasn't until I was sitting in front of Tom Cantrell— We were at an event, and it was after the event we went to go off and eat supper, and I was sitting at the end of the table. Tom was in a wheelchair, so that's why we were at the end. And we were just talking, and I just happened to feel a lot of love and content and just feel really good inside, and I ended up listening to Tom as he was speaking, and as he was speaking, all of a sudden, I see a bigfoot come out of his head. Now, I was thinking, what the hell did I just see? So I— Quick, I turned away, 'cause I thought, I can't believe I just saw this. So I looked again, and it was still there, so I looked away, and I thought, *Jena! You look right now!* You know, 'cause you gotta sometimes talk yourself into it. If you're afraid, you just say, take care of it. So, you know, I was ready to look back at it, and when I looked back at it, it was still there. And I was still very scared inside. I couldn't believe what I was seeing. It wasn't even about seeing Bigfoot so much as *how* it came through. And it wasn't up until that moment that I thought—that I realized that inter-dimensional is a reality. And you know, traveling interdimensionaly is a reality. And I never— I always thought about it, but not until that moment did I ever think that it was real.

JK: The way that she saw it though; it was like Tom's forehead was here, and it was like it peeked out from Tom's—like its head started to tilt forward out of Tom's head. Just to show—'cause Tom's into mind-speak and things like that, and, Jena, I know you had in your mind— You know, there's always— Even though we have psychic abilities, you still question everybody else's stuff until you experience it for yourself.

JG: Yes.

JK: That's just the rational part of the mind, and it just is. But I think that was in relation to—in answer to your question, "Is this mindspeak? Is the Bigfoot really talking to him?" And it's showing itself, peeking out at you.

JG: You say it so sweetly. In my mind, when I heard that, I was like, okay, all right...

JG: But I love Tom. I really love Tom, so I didn't care, you know. So that's why when it was a con, and that's pretty much what it was, it was a confirmation to me that that was real. And the coolest thing about it was the forehead. Now, this was the thing that really stood out to me. I don't know why I was drawn to the forehead, but it was straight across, and I saw how its hair went back. It came out of the roots here, and it grew back. Instead of, you know, how our hair grows, and it comes down like this, all of it. It was like—shaped like this, the hair. But it was the hairline that was just straight across—that it stunned me so much that I couldn't make out the rest of the face, 'cause I was just stuck on the hairline. And I saw this part and the bone, but the hairline for some reason just completely got me. And I'm now realizing that I'm checking out every photograph to check out those hairlines to see if it matches what I saw. So... yeah.

JK: And Jena's just always loved Tom Cantrell.

JG: Oh, yeah.

JK: He's just a sweet man, ever since we met him. So, I really think that was in reaction to your questioning it inside of yourself. He was showing himself to you just so you would understand that this is for real and it's a possibility and it's also available to us; we just need to tap into that connection within ourselves. That's how I feel that meant.

JG: And, by the way, I did tell Tom that, so he did know that it wasn't real at first.

JG: So don't worry about it if you do go down that road, 'cause he knows.

JK: He knows, and he loves us.

JG: He does love us. He's wonderful. But the incredible fact— It took me two weeks just to accept how that came through like that. The whole fact that interdimensional travel—and you know I've talked to Jen and Tammy, but I talk to Jen a lot more, and she said she thinks that maybe it was more of, um...

JK: A psychic connection.

JG: No, you said uh... traveling...

JK: Astral?

JG: Yes, astral. You said maybe it was astral, and I just don't feel like it was astral. That was too solid. That was too... Sorry, you can go to the next question, sorry.

MQ: Okay, well, the last question is just, what is on the horizon for the She-Squatchers going forward? And, any final thoughts you all might have are welcome.

JK: Going forward, well, we've been working a lot on— Rather than going to events and traveling the country this year, we've been focusing on traveling, doing expeditions, and filming documentaries.

TT: And next year, we're going international.

JK: Yeah, we got invited out of the country to do a Bigfoot conference next year. We're really excited about that. Yeah, I have to get a passport now.

TT: I have one.

JG: Well, you could go now, Tammy.

JK: I've just gotta say that we've been really fortunate that people enjoy us and want to bring us to their location to share the things that they've found.

TT: Our presentation is a hundred percent everything that we've experienced, and we have to cut some things out now, 'cause it's getting too much. Cut the older stuff and just keep—

JK: The meat of it. But I think that's what people often say. They love our presentation because it's all about the things that we've found, and we share videos and pictures—

TT: As opposed to other people's presentations. Other people don't present their evidence. They talk about their views. They talk about what they think it is, the history. You know, whatever. But they never talk about their own personal experiences and share their knowledge and what they've learned and their photographs and their evidence. People don't do that. Or, if they do, they're very few. We are among the few people that actually share our evidence. Because the only way that we're all gonna do this and find all the information that we want is if we share what each one of us knows. All of us. Not just us She-Squatchers but all of the researchers. If we all just come together and be like, okay, well, I tried this, and this worked for me, and I got this evidence by doing that, you know, and learning from each other—that's how we're gonna get all the confirmation that we need. And I don't think it's gonna be from people up there, you know, saying, "If you pay me a bunch of money, I'll take you to my hot spot." ...You know, I just think that everybody needs to work together, and we'll find our way through it together.

JK: We come from— So, we all have a little—during different times of our journey together doing this, we've had different ideas of what Bigfoot is and what it's about, and, you know, we've represented it at some points in time—all the different camps of Bigfoot, whether they were flesh and blood or, you know, an undiscovered ape or an interdimensional being of some kind. We have had all of those views, and yet we work together without any disharmony at all. And we're all open to being wrong and finding out what it really is. ...And I think that if we can do it, everyone else can too. And that's one of the biggest messages I try to tell people—is that we can all get along. It doesn't matter what your beliefs are. We just get out there and figure it out together and be open minded.

TT: We don't have to agree on what it is, but that doesn't mean that anyone's point or view is any less valid that anyone else's. Because none of us know. Nobody knows a hundred percent for sure, because none of us has sat down and had that conversation with Bigfoot themselves. So until that point, we're all just learning together, we're all researchers, and, yes, we may have experiences, and we may know what we know, but that doesn't mean that any one of us is a hundred percent right. Because we don't know.

JG: I do think that in the future, AI may be causing a lot of issues as far as trust in real evidence. But when it comes down to it, the only real evidence is—like Jen said—is getting out there and finding it for yourself. And it's the only thing that we can tell them if they're questioning us, or— You know, some people have literally come up to me [...] and thinking that I would react in some way, I think. "I didn't even know you guys existed." Oh, well, not everybody does. Would you like to know about us? So, then they have the option. But, you know, we don't expect people to know who we are. We don't expect people to, you know...

TT: We don't expect to make anybody believe anything. We're just sharing our own experiences with you. We don't have to prove anything to anybody. If you want to know that Bigfoot exists, you have to experience it yourself. You're never gonna believe just because somebody else said so.

JG: And you're never too old. Guess what? You can do whatever you need to do; just have that fire. You just need the fire.

JK: And it doesn't take a lot of physical stamina to get out there. You can carry a hiking chair out in the woods and sit down and see what happens, see if you have some experiences. People do that. And you don't have to be in great physical shape to do that. So, I mean, everybody has abilities to do that for the most part. I mean, Tom gets out there, and he's in a wheelchair.

TT: Exactly. Very true.

JG: And not only that. It's healthy, and it gets you healthier every time you go out there. And I think the energy when you're out there really changes you as a human being. I mean, we're getting out there. All the stress is going off our shoulders because we're absorbing this beautiful energy—the trees, the grass, the fresh air, the beautiful sky, the stars we see at night.

JG: Okay, you can take it all, but I'm just saying it recharges everyone. And I think it's so important.

TT: It is important to be out in nature 'cause it does heal you.

JG: I may be a little Cinderella about it, but you know what?

The interview concluded with much fun and laughter among the group, a great example of the loving dynamic that they share. (Jena has been known to, off the top of her head, start singing a Bigfoot song as if she's a Disney princess). I urge people not to be put off by their often humorous and free-spirted approach to the search for Bigfoot, because they are out there doing the work and just don't see any need to be stone-faced and stoic about it. These ladies are a force to be reckoned with. Their psychic talents are for real. I have been in the field with them and experienced Bigfoot with them, and I feel blessed and privileged to have become their friend.

4

SASQUATCH RESEARCH ASSOCIATION

I first became familiar with the Sasquatch Research Association (SRA) of Minnesota when I looked into the repeated Bigfoot activity on the property of Randy Bauer near the town of Blackduck, and I made it the subject of my 2021 book, *Sasquatch Central*. When Randy first began finding evidence in 2014, he searched online for general information on Bigfoot in Minnesota and found the SRA. They were led then by Jim Hebb, who, after examining photos Randy had taken, responded, "Randy, you've got a squatch." It's kind of a funny line in retrospect and emblematic of the early days of that case, reminding me a little of the iconic line, "You're gonna need a bigger boat" from the movie *Jaws*, and, as it would turn out, there was more than one squatch on that property. The case is still ongoing today.

I didn't enter the picture until late 2019, at which time Jim Hebb had left the group to move on to other things, and the new leader was Todd Newby of the Twin Cities area. The other members hailed from throughout Minnesota, and I met several of them in group campouts at the Blackduck property. I found the group to be very experienced, with years of research, and well equipped with all the latest high-tech gadgets being used in the search for Bigfoot.

I found Todd to be a friendly and engaging man who came across as a serious intellectual but with a sense of humor. At the 2023 Minnesota Bigfoot Conference in Grand Rapids, he was asked to replace the famous researcher, Professor Jeff Meldrum, as a speaker after Meldrum had to drop out due to a health crisis. Todd began his presentation with a humorous impression of Meldrum's well-known manner of speaking about the "mid-tarsal break" in Bigfoot tracks. That made the audience laugh.

Todd responded to questions for this book in December 2023:

TODD NEWBY

MIKE QUAST: Can you describe how you came to join the SRA and how the BFRO might have been a factor?

TODD NEWBY: The SRA, or Sasquatch Research Association, was started by three originating members. All three were investigators with the BFRO [Bigfoot Field Researchers Organization] and decided to branch out and start a new group with different goals. They identified an opportunity with an organization that attempted to bring together the vast disparate groups all seemingly struggling with same constraint, availability of access to content. Their approach was to bring together the plethora of organizations, associations, chapters, teams, or whatever descriptor best fit a group that all shared a common interest. That being all things sasquatch.

This proved, as the saying goes, easier said than done. There was a rational reason for this, and that would be the groups actually don't have a vested interest in sharing or promoting content that actually would drive traffic away from them and to a "competing" group. Each of these groups put in time and effort to development, put up money for professional development, legal expenses, gathering teams, purchased equipment, etc. So this isn't a trivial amount of work that these groups have invested, so to actively come together and share content is counter to the work being done to start up a group.

Nevertheless, the SRA did and still does endeavor to bring groups together. Now, back to answering your actual question. I was asked to join at the inception as a researcher. I had been working with the originating members for several years, trusted their work, and agreed with the philosophy espoused by this new approach. My primary function as a researcher was to scout new locations for expeditions, vet reports as they were submitted, conduct witness interviews on plausible sightings, coordinate annual expeditions, or anything else the team needed me to do to advance the cause. After several years, one of the original members stepped down, and I was asked to fill that vacancy, which I gladly accepted.

MQ: Since very few of us in Bigfoot research do it professionally, in what field do you make your living?

TN: I've been working in the financial services industry for over thirty-six years. I started out in 1987 working in the Operations department of a small broker/dealer in San Diego and moved out to Minnesota in 1994. I've been working for a large national bank for the last twenty-eight years doing a wide variety of functions, with my priority focus on risk management.

MQ: Where have you found what you would call the best Bigfoot hotspots, and why so?

TN: This is an interesting topic. Well, we don't believe the sasquatches migrate, for several reasons, one being that there are plenty of sightings during the winter months, so they aren't walking from Minnesota to Florida and back again. This is obviously impossible just from the scale of distance. So, if they don't migrate, then where do they go, and why don't we have all these known hotspots everywhere around the country? We believe they have a fairly large home range, following locations where resources are abundant. This home range can be upwards of twenty to fifty miles or more.

So, let's take the Nemadji State Forest. It is, well, over twenty miles in distance from the north to the southern boundaries, so it's really vast. It has several trails meandering through the forest, but it also has impenetrable areas with thick bogs that are prime habitat. It's absolutely impossible to truly dig into that location and do some valuable research, just due to the immense amount of land in that area. We would need hundreds of people over many years to dedicate their time to do any quality research in just that one state forest. Additionally, if they leave the area going after different food sources, then we would just be there to research in areas that are completely devoid of squatches. It's really hit or miss, and just pure luck when we find an area that has activity or squatch signs.

Also, we think that squatches adapt their behavior to locations based on the type of human activity. For Nemadji, it has many ATV trails and is quite popular with people invading the area on week-ends, traversing the trails on their wheelers, making lots of noise, but not deviating from those trails. So we think the squatches pull back during the day and are quite active at night when the ATVs leave.

Another location where we have done a lot of research is the Solana State Forest. We've found so much evidence of squatches, but it is a very popular area for people, and we just can't seem to get them to interact with us. I've personally spent a dozen trips to the area, going all throughout the forest, and it's clear that the squatches just don't come around while we are there. I would consider Solana a hotspot, but I'm not planning on going back, because I believe the squatches don't want to deal with the humans, and they hang out waiting for them to leave.

Back to the topic of finding hotspots; this is extremely difficult because there are literally only two areas to research, public or private land. The public land as outlined above has many challenges, so the only other choice is private land, and there are so few spots that are, one, having activity, and two, are willing to report it and then allow research to be done on their land. This is where Randy is truly the golden ticket sought out by all research organizations. He is having activity and is willing to allow groups to come out and spend time there. Finding hotspots is truly one of the most frustrating aspects of squatching, and they only might be hot for a very short period of time.

MQ: Are there certain techniques you use in interviewing witnesses and in conducting fieldwork?

TN: We have developed a template for interviewing witnesses that is designed to allow the person to drive the conversation. Our intention is to let the witness tell their story and not ask leading questions. As an example, we would ask, "What was the shape of the head?" instead of asking if they saw a cone-shaped head. We also get them to break down the experience into small time segments. We want them to focus on as much detail as possible and encourage them to take their time, really look back and try to remember all aspects while recounting their interactions. I've done dozens of interviews, and each one is unique, and I try to remain flexible and see how the flow of the conversation goes while being as supportive as possible. Many times, the witness is reluctant to even talk, fearing ridicule, which I do my best to assuage early on. I try to put myself in their place, doing my best to visualize what they have experienced. Most of our reports are submitted initially through the website, and they provide a written account, so I will do as much background research as possible—things such as location, etcetera.

Regarding fieldwork, that is what I enjoy the most pertaining to this subject. Getting outdoors and being in the woods brings a level of happiness like no other. Before going to any location, I first do as much Google scouting as possible. I spend quite a while just reviewing aerial maps, looking for things such as ATV trails, any areas of bogs or lakes, ponds, and rivers. My favorite locations are as far away from homes or people as possible. Getting as deep into the woods and going off trail or bushwhacking; that is where the signs are going to be found.

Squatches may occasionally use trails or roads, but it isn't their primary focus, so getting off those areas utilized by humans is key. This activity does come with risks, so I make sure I'm prepared to go off trail by having a good quality GPS tracker to ensure I don't become lost in the dense forest, which has happened. I've relied upon that GPS to get me back to basecamp on many occasions. I also carry many tools of the trade, such as tape measure, rubber gloves, binoculars, bear spray, bug spray, water, camera, video camera, walkie talkie, a walking stick, just to name a few. As I go into the field, I try and absorb as much information as possible, checking out things I'm not familiar with and trying to learn something new even if it has no bearing on sasquatch at all. I'm always on the lookout for stick structures, footprints, scat, big boy trails, etcetera, and ninety percent of the time find absolutely nothing but couldn't be happier just being out. One technique I also try to employ is turning around and looking behind me on irregular intervals.

[Author's note: I do that too.]

MQ: Can you recount some of your most memorable experiences in the search for Bigfoot?

TN: My most memorable experience in the search for Bigfoot? My most memorable experience was a fifteen-minute sighting through a thermal imager at close range. This happened in 2012, near Moose Lake, Minnesota on private property. We had been going to this location for many years—a place called Heart Camp—due to the heart-shaped bog which was visible on Google Maps. I had a brief thermal sighting in the same location in 2009, but this one was fantastic. There were about eight of us there, and it was roughly 10:30 PM on a warm fall night. One of our team asked if anyone wanted to break out the toys, and I immediately said yes. I was given a thermal scope that had been retrofitted with a recording device. Back then, the thermals didn't record, so one of the guys in our group figured out how to make it work by attaching it to a large helmet. It was uncomfortable, but it worked.

I put it on and started scanning the woods. Seeing nothing, I started heading down the trail looking west. I almost immediately picked up a heat signature down the trail. I called over to have someone else have a look and passed the helmet to him. He didn't see anything and handed the helmet back to me and said, "If you pick it up again, keep your eye on it because it is recording" and went back to the fire with the rest of the team. I looked back down the trail and picked up the signature again exactly in the same location. It stayed there for several minutes and then began to move towards the camp, off the trail in the woods. I was able to follow it as it got closer and closer. I could only see a round shape, not an entire body.

I continued toward the camp, when I lost sight of it, so I moved back to camp to reposition myself and see if I could pick it back up. One of the guys in camp was playing a Native flute, and it was heading directly toward him, when I lost it in the dense woods. I scanned the area behind the guy playing the flute but didn't see anything, so I went back down the trail to my original position. After a short period, I was able to pick it back up as it was now moving away from the camp, going back to the direction it came from. I continued to watch as it went back to the spot where I first saw it, and it stayed there for about ten minutes and then moved where I couldn't see it any longer. I went back to the camp, where I spent the rest of the night telling everyone the story, over and over, because I just couldn't believe how cool it was to witness that rare occurrence.

The next morning, we scouted the path it took, finding a small trail but no footprints or broken tree branches. I went back to my spot where I saw the whole thing, and one guy who is six-three stood on the trail, but I couldn't see him. He took off his shirt and had to wave it over his head for me to see where he was. At that point, I saw a stand of trees between me and the trail and found them to top out at eight feet. The thermal image I saw was above those trees, so I was only seeing the head, which was the round object. When then went to download the files off the helmet camera, and all three files were blank. Nothing recorded. So the curse of technology and sasquatch struck again. I only have my memory of the entire encounter, but I will never forget seeing that bright object in the thermal scope, above the trees, coming towards our camp and moving away. It moved so smoothly too, not bobbing up and down, just straight in and out. That was the same weekend we found the spiral fractures on the deer hind legs, so it was a fantastic weekend.

MQ: What is it that motivates you in your search for Bigfoot, and do you have an end goal in mind?

TN: I really don't have an endgame in mind. I would love to have a close daylight sighting, but I think that is the same for basically everyone that goes out and looks. At this point, I've been doing this for over a decade and what really motivates me is to get outside with the people I love and see what we can find. If we find something, fantastic. If we don't, oh well. If I could script it, I would probably say that, if I could find a body that died from natural causes and get it in the hands of credible scientists, that would be pretty cool. Not only would I be able to tell all my non-believer friends "told ya so," but it might spur on a lot more research on the topic.

MQ: With all your experience, what is your opinion on whether Bigfoot is a flesh and blood animal or if there might be some kind of paranormal element involved?

TN: I think this is an appropriate end point and will say that it is my stance that there isn't any evidence that I've seen that would lead me to believe they aren't anything more than flesh and blood creatures. The question of whether they might be some type of human or ape or any other primate— I really don't have an opinion. With that said, I have had things that have happened to me that I currently cannot explain, but just because that is the case doesn't mean they are anything supernatural. I just can't make that leap, as it seems to me to stop the conversation. If we don't know what something is, I think it's convenient to slap a paranormal label on it and be done with it. That seems intellectually lazy to me. Don't give up and make a proclamation which has no semblance in facts and walk away. Keep digging, keep researching, keep thinking and figure it out. It will probably take minds much smarter than mine to ultimately figure out this seemingly endless riddle, but that won't stop me from playing along. I enjoy the topic and will continue doing it as long as that is the case.

JOHN BADGER

 John Badger, 55, is a member of the SRA who has formed a good friendship with Randy Bauer and has visited his property near Blackduck more than any other member, witnessing some dramatic and bizarre activity along the way. Hailing from Cloquet, Minnesota, he comes across as a true rugged outdoorsman.

John did a recorded interview for this book in late winter 2023, which turned a bit more conversational than most:

MIKE QUAST: Can you describe how you came to join the SRA, and, if applicable to original members, how the BFRO might have been a factor?

JOHN BADGER: I really joined the SRA when a group of ex-BFRO members were looking to form a new group. They had been kind of a loose-knit group after they quit the BFRO, and I had met some of the members at the time that had been in the BFRO at the filming of season two of *Finding Bigfoot*. I eventually hooked up with them, and we just did some loose research and stuff like that and some outings, and then there were roughly four guys that formed the SRA and put together an organization, and a bunch of us joined it kind of as a core member group, and then other people that weren't part of our group could also join and come on expeditions and so forth. The BFRO was actually something that I was following, so I always was interested in the Bigfoot subject but wasn't really involved with anything until a buddy of mine asked if I wanted to come see the BFRO and *Finding Bigfoot* filming in Wright, Minnesota. And at that point, I realized how many people had relatives or friends that had seen or witnessed at the filming, so I decided to get a little more involved. So, I guess that's kind of how it all happened.

MQ: Where have you found what you would call the best Bigfoot hotspots, and why so?

JB: Well, Blackduck is one of the areas that I felt was the most active, and I guess the person whose house I've been going to, Randy, has everything that works well with it. It's got powerlines, it's got water, a lot of state land, limited access to other people using the property, so I think the activity that he's had and the stuff that I feel is going on all relates to what we have all kind of known, that they use powerlines as corridors and waterways for drinking and food sources and so forth like that, and just the remoteness and the lack of people using the property. And he's got a lot of trails cut through the woods. I think they're used by most animals, including sasquatch. Another area I feel is very active is gonna be the Nemadji River valley. Kind of St. Croix—that area. Kind of border of Wisconsin and Minnesota. There's been a lot of stories down there. I haven't spent a lot of time in there, but I've heard it's quite remote. There's a lot of state land, a lot of water. Again, things that require a larger animal to have in territory. Another area would be the Remer area, which I feel is very active because it's bordered by just massive amounts of wetlands and uninhabited areas. It runs all the way up toward Ball Club-Six Mile Lake area. And I think because there have been a number of sightings in that area, I think that's just a really big hot spot. Otherwise, I think a lot of parts of northern Minnesota, areas that are less inhabited, you know—north of the Iron Range, Boundary Waters, all the way over into Koochiching County, south of International Falls.

MQ: Are there certain techniques you use in interviewing witnesses and conducting fieldwork?

JB: Well, interviewing witnesses has generally been— A lot of it's been oral. We did follow with the SRA a certain set of questions that are on a sheet of paper that we kept where with all the sightings we could compare location, date, time, the certain things that were just customary to the sighting or experience logged, and then after that, a lot of it was open-ended questions. Could you describe what you saw? The hair? Did you see a face, movement, walking? Was it crouching? The color of the hair, and so forth like that. A lot of times, it was just letting the person talk and giving us their experience after we got the basics asked. So that was kind of how we would interview witnesses. We had other members in the group that did a lot of interviewing as well, so a lot of times, I was with or along. And fieldwork, a lot of it. We had different people. We had one guy that was really good with scat. Some people were really good at looking up tracks. Big thing with fieldwork was that some of it was done more scientifically; other stuff was just getting out in the field and just looking for evidence, maybe tree snaps, breaks.

Footprints were always paramount, you know. If there was a sighting, we would also follow trails that we felt we found prints on, and stuff like that. For instance, one of the things that happened was where we found a kill zone where something was ambushed, killed a deer, and we went back, and we were able to follow the tracks and where the blood had been coming out of the deer on the left or the right side, depending on which side it was being carried, and we followed it as far as we could. We were able to judge the distance of the tracks and of the impressions that were left by the animal that was carrying it and so forth. Things like that—take a lot of measurements, record stuff, so that we could determine stride length. If it went over a fence line, we were able to judge, you know—did it go through it, around, or above it? Whatever. There were certain things you could tell by the matting on both sides of the fence. A lot of the research was based on just fieldwork, just us getting out and backing up the sightings with evidence if we could, hair samples if we could find them. Randy did a good job of getting hair into some labs.

MQ: Can you recount some of your most memorable experiences in the search for Bigfoot?

JB: Well, I'd say my sighting was one of the most memorable. That's when there were a couple of us out at Randy's because it was getting to be dusk, and we were walking out. We were actually gonna go walk back to the state land. And on the way to the state land, we were walking the fence line. The ground was uneven, so we were kind of talking and walking, looking down at our feet a lot, because they mowed the grass around the fence line level, but underneath, there were boulders that had been bulldozed out. So we're making our way along the fence line to the east, and there's a rise in the hill where the fence goes up, and you can see a cut where the trees are on both sides and then the open sky. It wasn't too dark to see, but it was getting close to that point. Seventy percent of the light you could see still. And Mike had been using his therm. He was looking up a little bit at the fence line, but then he quit using it, and we were walking, and I happened to just look up, and from the right to the left, I watched what I can describe as an extremely large, black, very fast moving, upright humanlike figure running. And it took two long steps and then one leap over the top of the fence line, which was fifty-four inches, barbed wire, and clear it like what I could only describe as like a hurdler, so the body was upright, the front leg was out and the back leg was back like you would hurdle it in track. And it landed on the other side, took one more step, and it was gone. And the speed was far faster than any human I've ever seen. And I knew it wasn't a deer, because deer are on four legs, and they don't have an upright body when they go over the fence. It wasn't a black bear, because usually black bears, for the most part, go through the fence, usually the bottom strands, which we found later on through multiple conclusions of walking the fence line. There were multiple areas where bears would go underneath the fence or at least through the first couple of strands, leaving a lot of hair. After seeing one go over a fence and just come to be running at full sprint and then leap like that and have an upright posture— It leads me to believe—and I had no other explanation—it wasn't human. It wasn't bear. It wasn't deer. It can only lead to one thing, because there were multiple sightings at Randy's already.

MQ: Right. Could you hear the footsteps too? Were there really heavy footfalls as this thing ran, and then when it hit the ground after it jumped?

JB: I couldn't. I don't remember our exact distance, but it was far enough away that we couldn't hear the footsteps or any sound, but I know I asked Mike. You know, at first, I'm shocked. We're both carrying something in our hands to record, but you know, my first reaction was like, "What the...? What was that that I just saw?" My heart just started pounding. It was an instant fight or flight type feeling. Something large that I'm not used to seeing in the woods just ran across this fence line, and not knowing, I thought Mike had seen it too, but he had been looking down as we were walking, and by the time I even blurted anything out, it had already disappeared into the woods. It was fast. And I said, "Did you see that, Mike?" and he said, "No, what?" and I said, "Oh my god, I think I just saw a bigfoot jump the fence. And we went up there, and we investigated, but that year, it was pretty dry, and it had come through a grassy area on both sides of the fence, so we followed the uncut grass like a trail, so we didn't know if it had veered off into the woods or if it followed that trail that went perpendicular to the actual fence line.

We didn't find any hair at that point on the top of the fence line. Now, Randy did go back and said he found some strands on the top, so I believe he collected those. He also went back because I had to leave that next day, and that was the day that he went out there, and he had an airplane that was flying around that came from Bemidji that was circling at treetop level right in that area, and Randy watched it. So, somebody was alerted to it somehow, and I had only sent the coordinates to one person, so it was kind of an interesting coincidence that there would have been a plane that flew there from Bemidji, came right to that location, circled three or four times right over that spot, and then went all the way back. I did go back there and reenact it. When I had more time, I came back a couple of weeks from there, and I brought a refrigerator box, and I had Randy go down to where I saw it go over the fence, and I had him hold up the box. And I kept telling him higher, higher. So I realized that this thing was bigger than I thought it was because of the distance. That made it even more incredible to me now, because if it was something like a deer or a bear, I wouldn't have been able to see the size that I saw from that distance as he's holding that up, because in order for it to go over that fence it was way higher than the fence. So I would say it was at least double the height of the fence. So that's fifty-four inches, you know, so it was at least another fifty-four inches above that. So that thing was big.

MQ: Yeah, I remember being there that night. I was back at the campfire, and when you got back and were telling about it, I remember I asked you, "Do you think it's possible it was the ten-footer that Randy has seen a few times?" and you said yes, basically.

JB: Yeah. And that just confirmed it when we went back and measured the feet. Because something with legs and then from the waist up was above that fence line, you know it had to be huge.

MQ: What is it that motivates you in your search for Bigfoot, and do you have an end goal in mind?

JB: I'm always looking for answers. I guess I got interested in this only because of people I knew personally that swear that there was something that they saw and were avid hunters and outdoorsmen and were incredible to me—so a search for knowing it myself. I have a high curiosity level, and I need to get the answers for things. A lot of people say it's not science based, but that's how science works. Science is based on looking for facts, looking for evidence, searching for new things. That's what science is, versus anthropology looking at things that have already been here. So, I had a high curiosity level and was just looking for answers, and I thought the best way to do that is put myself in a situation that would allow me to do that, and to talk to more people that have experienced it and find a commonality of those experiences, to see if there was something that tied every-thing together. Certain behaviors, certain characteristics. And the end goal would be— Well, it was to actually have a sighting. But the end goal would be actually to find evidence that would be convincing to the skeptical public. I think there's been a lot of evidence presented, but there may be a dead body or remains of a recently deceased one. I'm not sure if photographic evidence is gonna do it with AI-generated stuff.

MQ: Now some researchers say that they're not out to prove anything to anyone else, they just want to learn as much as they can for themselves, but when it comes to that final proof, that's gonna solve the mystery once and for all. Would you say you would like to be a part of that if you could?

JB: Yeah, I think I'd like to. If there's some stuff that I could get out there, I definitely would. For me, I've already seen one, and that belief — I can reconfirm it, I guess, by seeing it a second and third time, but I more, like, just want to learn the habits of what they do and where they go. That's just more of my curiosity as to getting more answers as to how these things operate day and night. I know people that don't believe and are not gonna be convinced regardless, but ultimately, if there's a body examined by the real scientific community...

MQ: Okay, the last question is, with all your experience, what is your opinion on whether Bigfoot is a flesh and blood animal or if there might be some kind of paranormal element involved?

JB: Well, I've always been a flesh and blood guy, so I guess to me, if it exists, it's still an animal that lives, that breathes, that has abilities to avoid human conflicts, avoid human presence. But there's things that I can't explain, which lead me to believe there might be more to this, so I'm open-minded. So, the thought that there might be a— especially with Randy's place, where tracks can stop and end, and they're definitely tracks. That's a mystery to me, and I would like to find out more about that. Is there two things going on, or is it the same thing, or what?

MQ: I guess I'd kind of like to take this opportunity to bring up the sighting with you and Randy in the deer stand when you guys saw the portal and the orbs that came out of it, and as Randy tells the story, these orbs morphed into bigfoots and, you know, he's always saying, "It wasn't only me that saw this. John Badger was there, and he saw it too." You've kind of seemed to downplay it a little more than he does. Would you say that's just because he had a better view of what was going on than you did because of your position in the stand?

JB: Correct, yeah. That's the part that draws me away from flesh and blood a little bit, because what we saw shimmering in that dark area, and like you said, the orbs—and I seen the orbs, so I don't know what those represent. I'm curious about that, you know. I've watched them walking with my naked eye. And they seem to have coincided with that night [...] [Randy had] more of a better vantage point than I did, maybe, but we did both see what he described. He saw more of the Bigfoot kind of morphing into whatever allegedly it was than I could. But, you know, you're focusing your eyes in a dark environment on certain things. We're both looking at bigger things that happened, so he may have seen a little more than I did, definitely. But what he saw and we both saw together— We both had similar experiences, and he had somewhat little more additional experience of seeing stuff. But that's the part that leads me to believe that, being a flesh and blood guy, there's a little more to this mystery than I think.

CHRISTOPHER SAM

Chris Sam is a former Marine who lives in Clear Lake, Minnesota, just north of the Twin Cities area, who brings a Native American perspective to his work searching for Bigfoot with the SRA. He responded to questions for this book in April of 2024.

MIKE QUAST: Can you describe how you came to join the SRA, and, if applicable to original members, how the BFRO might have been a factor?

CHRIS SAM: I believe I am one of the original members of the

SRA. I was a BFRO investigator here in Minnesota with Kris Perlock, Jim Hebb, and Andy Pieper. When those three broke away from the BFRO and formed the SRA, I decided to follow them on their new endeavor, because I had been on several BFRO expeditions with them and enjoyed hanging out with them. Jim Hebb is now one of my best friends. I found the BFRO was a personality cult, with the favored investigators getting all the good gear and tips. I've never done well in those types of situations, so it was easy for me to leave the BFRO. I had some great experiences and opportunities due to my affiliation with the BFRO. I hold no ill will towards the BFRO; it just wasn't for me.

MQ: Since very few of us in Bigfoot research do it professionally, in what field do you make your living?

CS: I am in federal human resources—twenty-six-plus years—across three different federal agencies.

MQ: Where have you found what you would call the best Bigfoot hotspots, and why so?

CS: There is a spot in the Paul Bunyan State Forest in Hubbard County, Minnesota that is my all-time favorite. I learned about it as a BFRO investigator, after a local resident reported a fourteen-foot track in a dirt road near his house. This is where I heard samurai chatter, and it is also where Jim Hebb got his photo of "Minnesota Red." I ran a BFRO expedition in this location and have had many squatchy experiences there. I haven't been there in a few years, as it's a long trip from where I used to live—Minneapolis—and just not feasible to spend a lot of time traveling there. There was also a spot in Kettle River referred to as the Aho property that was a great spot, as the family that lived there had many sightings and experiences. This was where Andy Pieper recorded his sasquatch howls that were analyzed on the first *Finding Bigfoot* Minnesota episode. Unfortunately, access to the area is very limited because it is private property. I had an experience in this area where I was using a pair of military-grade night vision goggles, and I watched a coyote walk to within fifteen feet of me as I was standing on a bridge over a gurgling creek. It was rainy that night, probably 2:30 AM, and I was wearing a full rain suit with a hood. I'm convinced the coyote mistook me for a sasquatch, because I watched the coyote come through the woods, stick its head through the weeds on the edge of the road, and look right at me standing on the bridge. It then came up out of the ditch and trotted right towards me on the bridge. It stopped abruptly about fifteen feet from me, I believe because it abruptly realized I wasn't a sasquatch. It then took off like a shot through the woods. Randy Bauer's place has taken over as my number one spot. I have had several strange occurrences there, not necessarily attributable to sasquatch.

MQ: Are there certain techniques you use in interviewing witnesses and in conducting fieldwork?

CS: I have come to rely heavily on my ability to read people to help determine credibility. I also like to take in the totality of the evidence before making a determination. For example, if investigating a photo, I will ask to see the photos immediately before and after the photo being analyzed to see what is shown there. Many times, the person cannot or would not produce them, which would lead me to question the validity of the photo.

MQ: Can you recount some of your most memorable experiences in the search for Bigfoot?

CS: My most memorable was hearing "samurai chatter" in the woods at 11:30 at night. It sounded like a man speaking Japanese in the woods, but there was no way a man would have been in the woods at that particular location and time speaking Japanese loud enough that me and four other people could hear it. I have also heard strange howls mixed in with a pack of coyotes going off. The first howls were to the north of me. Another pack then sounded off to the south of me with the same strange howl mixed in. It was wonderful and exciting hearing this, until I realized I was in between the two.

MQ: What is it that motivates you in your search for Bigfoot, and do you have an end goal in mind?

CS: Initially, my goal was to see a sasquatch in the wild, which I have, and it was just to satisfy my own personal curiosity. I've never felt the need to prove the existence of sasquatch to others. Frankly, I couldn't care less if a person believes in sasquatch or not. Being Native—enrolled member of the Mille Lacs Band of Ojibwe Indians —I grew up knowing these creatures exist and incorporated them into my belief system. Researching was purely to satisfy my own curiosity. I became addicted to the research and learned a lot in a very short period of time. I do not have an end goal. I guess if I did, it would have been a visual sighting, which I've already had. As of now, I continue researching to experience new things with these creatures. I've already seen enough to prove to myself that they do exist.

MQ: With all your experience, what is your opinion on whether Bigfoot is a flesh and blood animal or if there might be some kind of paranormal element involved?

CS: I believe it has a paranormal aspect to it. I use the term paranormal here in the strictest sense, as in being beyond human understanding, not some magic being that exists both in the spiritual and physical realms—although my Native side believes this. I believe the creature is able to somehow manipulate its vibration and pass between physical dimensions. Ron Morehead calls this his Quantum Bigfoot theory. This has put me at odds with others in the SRA, as their official position is that it's a flesh and blood animal. I've always been of the opinion that until we understand exactly what sasquatch is, we have to entertain all theories. Think about our vision. The range of what we can see is very limited, which means there is much we cannot see. Conversely, the range of human hearing is very limited as well, meaning there is much we cannot hear. We don't know what we don't know about this world. Hell, we can't even figure out how the Egyptian pyramids were constructed. Ha-ha!

Well, I think I've said everything I want to say. Thanks, Mike, for the opportunity to contribute to your project.

ANDY PIEPER

 Andy Pieper, 54, declined to be interviewed for this book but did consent to being included in the narrative. Living in Lakeville, Minnesota, a suburb of the Twin Cities, he is employed in the computer software field and owns his own business called TaleSpinner Minis, in which he designs and creates all kinds of miniature figures from the realm of sci-fi, fantasy, etc. There is an intense intellectualism to him, which he directs in his spare time toward the study of Bigfoot. Within the Bigfoot field, he is best known for having captured an audio recording in March of 2012 in the Moose Lake-Kettle River area of Carlton County that is popularly known online as the "Minnesota Howls." Captured in an area known for several Bigfoot encounters, it features the howling of distant wolves and then seemingly something else with a much deeper voice that joins in with a howl that does not seem to be a wolf but something mysterious. This recording was the inspiration for the Animal Planet TV show, *Finding Bigfoot*, to come to the area and film the fourth episode of their second season, the first of three Minnesota episodes they would feature in their nine-season run.

I met Andy in September of 2020, when he and several other members of the SRA took part in a weekend expedition to the property of Randy Bauer near Blackduck in Beltrami County, where Bigfoot activity has been going on for several years. During that weekend, Andy and his teenage son were lucky enough to have not just one but two creature sightings: one very quick glimpse during daylight, and then another under the darkness of night in which a gigantic black figure crossed a trail directly in front of them and emitted such a foul odor that it made them feel sick. Andy bid farewell to that weekend by telling Randy that his place was the "squatchiest I've ever seen."

I was part of that weekend expedition too and had my own experiences, and I'm glad for Andy to have been a part of it.

5
———————

ITASCA COUNTY BIGFOOT RESEARCH

In my ongoing investigations at the Randy Bauer site near Blackduck, with its frequent Bigfoot activity, I became aware of a small research group called Itasca County Bigfoot Research, a three-man team consisting of friends, Zac Malmquist, Jeremy Olson, and Matt Aultman. Though based in Itasca County in northern Minnesota where there are many Bigfoot reports, they do not limit their searching to that county but expand out into surrounding areas. I met Zac and Jeremy at Randy's place in Beltrami County in May 2023, when they had heard about it and wanted to check it out. I found them to be fairly young, rugged outdoorsmen who had invested a lot into their search for Bigfoot and employed expensive equipment such as a drone that they flew over the area to capture aerial footage over several miles. Though it didn't detect anything of interest, I had to admire their efforts.

On May 23, 2023, Zac Malmquist responded, apparently on behalf of the group, to a series of questions I submitted by email to all the members.

MIKE QUAST: Can you describe how you came to join Itasca County Bigfoot Research?

ZAC MALMQUIST: For a few years, a couple friends and I would get together to go squatching. We didn't really take it very seriously until the spring of 2022, when we started to get some unusual reports. We noticed that there wasn't really a community presence for Itasca County, so we hatched the idea of a Facebook group page to field reports, and through it, the ICBR was created.

MQ: Where have you found what you would call the best Bigfoot hotspots, and why so?

ZM: We have been fielding reports north of Grand Rapids, Minnesota. Basically, anywhere in the Chippewa National Forest has promise. We have researched a few areas in the Balsam Township area, as well as Soumi Hills and various areas outside of Bigfork. In short, the more remote, the better.

MQ: Are there certain techniques you use in interviewing witnesses and conducting fieldwork?

ZM: As for interviews, we try to let it flow naturally. Being that we were born and raised up here, we try and tap into that local vibe. Get people talking about day to day up here, how the weather is, how annoying those city people coming up here are, etcetera. It usually gets them to open up. As for fieldwork, I think the major key we use is always, "Can you explain what you just saw in other ways?" For example, if we come across stick structures. We will look at it and see if we can determine the source of where those sticks came from, if it makes sense that they could have fallen into place naturally. And if it's not natural, we look at other factors. Could a bunch of kids have made this? Is it an old shelter for a hunter or a lost hiker? Basically, looking at all the possible explanations for it, as well as looking for secondary evidence to support the claim that this was Sasquatch. To say the least, we are very critical of the evidence provided to us. We have tried game cameras with no real luck. Also have started to leave trinkets like marbles to visit at later dates. Leaving apples and peanut butter to attract attention as well. Personally, I am not above talking out loud to whatever is listening when out in the woods.

MQ: Can you recount some of your most memorable experiences in the search for Bigfoot?

Zac Malmquist (L) and Jeremy Olson (R)

ZM: Spring of 2022, we were out in a remote private location in Balsam Township for a weekend. I got the idea to go out on a solo mission late afternoon. There was a rather large cedar swamp about a quarter mile from our camp location. I wanted to sit there and observe for a while. After a few minutes, I pulled out my camera with plans to make a video, panning through the swamp I was looking at. It was at that moment I heard sticks flying through the air and landing somewhere behind me. I thought for sure that this was Jeremy or Matt messing with me. We enjoy the research, but we are all good friends and are not above pulling practical jokes on each other. Well, I looked around and didn't see them, nor did I hear any footsteps of anyone getting closer. So I sat quiet for the next few minutes just listening for whatever, waiting for my friends to complete their practical joke on me and come jumping out from behind a tree. It never came, so I pulled my camera out a second time, and the exact same thing happened. I hear the sound of sticks flying by and landing somewhere behind me. At this point, I got the feeling that whatever was going on, whatever was doing that, didn't want me there and certainly didn't want me recording. So, I picked myself up and hastily walked back to the campsite. There, I found Jeremy and Matt sitting around a campfire proclaiming they hadn't moved from the spot. This shook me a little as it dawned on me that

97

this could possibly be a sasquatch messing with me. So after I collected myself, Jeremy and I headed back out there. We found an impression on the side of a hill that was about sixteen inches long. The spot was forward and to the right compared to where I was sitting, a place that something or someone could have concealed themselves well only to pop out and hurl sticks in my direction. That was certainly a wakeup call that we just might be onto something.

MQ: What is it that motivates you in your search for Bigfoot, and do you have an end goal in mind?

ZM: I grew up in Balsam Township. Just a small community with a gas station. By the age of fifteen, I had several encounters with black bears. Some right in front of me in a standoff, proclaiming they are getting that bacon that was just cooked. To say the least, I was not afraid of them. But one summer day, I was walking down the road that led behind my parents' house and caught the flash of something large and reddish brown moving through the woods. I looked over to see this creature walking on two legs. I don't know if it had seen me at this time, as it was rapidly moving away from me, but I didn't care. I was so scared that I ran as fast as I could back to the house and locked the doors. I talked a little about it to my parents and friends, but it was more or less excused for something else. "Oh, you probably saw a bear or a moose and just scared yourself." I went with it, even though in the back of my mind, I knew I had seen something that wasn't a known creature. Once I was older, I started to joke about it, saying I once saw Bigfoot. Just more of a jest to friends than anything serious about it. But then I found myself out at a Bigfoot museum in northern California. I started to talk to the owner of the place, and I mentioned my story. To my surprise, he actually took what I was saying seriously. It was the first time anyone had done that, and it really made me think that maybe there was some validity to what I saw. To me, the end goal is to experience them, understand them better. I don't need to be the guy that proves their existence. I want to validate what I saw at fifteen and maybe share that experience with a few others.

MQ: With all your experience, what is your opinion on whether

Bigfoot is a flesh and blood animal or if there might be some kind of paranormal element involved?

ZM: Once I really started to sit down and research this subject, reading various books, watching countless movies and podcasts, I started to pick up on a couple themes. Most encounters were extremely short with the creature just disappearing. They would walk into the forest or go over a hill, and that was it. No more sightings. You never hear reports of people actually following these creatures after the first sighting of them. Second theme is, when you hear about tracks, they all just start in a spot and stop after a while. They never lead back to a den or a cave. Just starting in one spot and stopping in another. And finally, if you start to look at what the caloric intake of a large creature is like, you have to wonder why we haven't been able to find more hard evidence of them. Bears in general do not like to be around people, but in their search for food, they will expose themselves to knock over garbage cans in neighborhoods. We don't seem to see that with Sasquatch.

Overall, all of these factors have led me to believe that there is certainly something paranormal about them. There has to be. There is no way such a large creature can be this elusive in our northern woods without having some sort of secret that we just don't understand. And I think when we understand that secret and learn how to observe it/measure it, I think that is when we will finally have solid proof of their existence.

6

OTHERS

DOUG HAJICEK

Minnesota is fortunate to be the home of one of the most high-profile and industrious figures in the field of cryptozoology. Living today in the city of Blaine, a suburb of Minneapolis, Doug Hajicek (pronounced high-check) is a veteran wildlife researcher, filmmaker, television producer, inventor, entrepreneur, and, most recently, publisher. In his mid-sixties now, he is best known as the producer of the hit show, *Monster Quest*, which was engineered by his production company, Whitewolf Entertainment, and aired for four seasons on the History Channel from October 2007 to March 2010.

It dealt with all manner of cryptozoological creatures, from known species in unusual situations to the figures of legends whose very existence is in dispute, including a number of episodes on Bigfoot. It brought tremendous attention to the subject and was, in my opinion, probably the best television series ever to deal with cryptozoology. In the course of producing it, Doug designed and created some sophisticated camera rigs in the effort to capture evidence of various creatures. Prior to this, Doug also produced the in-depth documentary, *Sasquatch: Legend Meets Science*, which first aired on the Discovery Channel on January 9, 2003. Because of his many endeavors, Doug has been able to bring considerable financial resources to the field that so fascinates him.

My own association with Doug came about when I began to investigate the ongoing Bigfoot activity at the Randy Bauer property near Blackduck, Minnesota in 2020. Randy reached out to many sources in trying to understand what was happening around his home, including Doug, who became interested and involved in the case. At this same time, he became interested in entering the publishing field and giving up-and-coming authors a chance to showcase their material. Once we connected, I was surprised when he generously offered to take my previously self-published books on Bigfoot in Minnesota and have professional editions of them produced at no cost to me. The book on Randy's case I was working on at the time, *Sasquatch Central: High Strangeness at a Northern Minnesota Homestead*, was one of the first to be published by Doug's new company, Hangar 1 Publishing, which he operates with his son, Alex.

Doug responded to a series of questions for this book in November 2023:

MIKE QUAST: How did you first become interested in cryptozoology in general and Bigfoot in particular?

DOUG HAJICEK: I was a curious kid who gravitated to any mysteries. My father read me Charles Fort books at bedtime by my request. My parents were never negative on these topics, but rather open and neutral. On a hunting trip in the late seventies, early eighties, my Uncle Jack, who I was close to, invited me on a deer hunting trip to Ore, Minnesota in a real wilderness setting. It was me and my cousins and my best friend, Ron. Jack put us all on a deer stand about a half mile apart. I ended up on a deer stand that was so beautiful with thick green moss—a small creek lined with ferns. It was a true Fae forest. It was dark when I settled in to my stand on a cold crisp morn, about 4:30 AM. After some time sitting silent, the sun rose and brightened the sky in a deep blue color. I heard what sounded like chest beating. This was so loud, I could feel it in my body. It was so bassy, I knew it wasn't a grouse, as I had heard this common drumming many times. This was thunderous. Okay, so it was just an odd thing at this point, that is until I was hit with a powerful smell that was gagging. I am smelling rotten meat—sweet, sickly, rich, rotten food like one would smell on the streets of New Orleans the day after Mardis Gras on a hot day. It was extremely gagging as I covered my nose so I could filter the stench a bit. Then the smell and the chest beating ended as quickly as it had started. I was relieved and confused at the same time. I had not associated the stink to Bigfoot, but I did the chest beating to a gorilla.

The day dragged on uneventful and without seeing a big buck that I wanted. We were all supposed to meet at a predetermined spot, for lunch at noon, that was basically in the center of all these well-placed and sturdy deer stands. I made my way back to base camp, and the first topic was how my cousin had had a similar experience, as did my youngest cousin, and my uncle had the experience. My cousin blurted out how he felt we had all been visited by a bigfoot. It made sense, I guess, as it may have explained the whole thing in one neat package. My first experience opened my mind to bigfoots maybe living in Minnesota, and I had possibly been witness to some intimidation. I will never know for sure.

Years later, I partnered with Ron Schara to produce a magazine-style outdoor TV special and later a series. It was on one of these wilderness stories I was producing, I found myself at an arctic lake fishing big trophy trout of thirty pounds or more. It was here I saw in the Windy River on Nueltin Lake a massive lake trout slowly going after a big lake trout I was reeling in. The trout I saw, I can only describe as being as big as a man in the water. When I got home, I was obsessed in getting footage of a monster trout in its natural habitat. Next thing I knew, I was at Selwyn Lake even farther north with an array of big lures. One had a camera built into it. It was on this trip that a pee break brought us to shore, and we saw huge footprints coming out of the shallow water in this bay on the damp sand beach. They were huge humanlike footprints, approximately fourteen to sixteen inches. I was with a number of other people, and we followed the tracks into damp pea gravel, where the prints were still deep. In fact, Rick, who was close to 300 pounds, jumped off a raised rock and did not dent the soil. We continued to follow the straight line of tracks to a small stand of stunted black spruce trees, and what I saw shocked me... A footprint in front of the trunk of a seven- to ten-foot spindly tree and one print directly behind it. This meant one thing: the creature that made these tracks stepped over the tree. I remember Rick saying we need to leave *now*. I managed to lead the group past the trees and could see the tracks going across the rolling tundra. I knew they were not bear tracks—double-step tracks, but no claws, broad heel, and the perfect shape of the foot of a heavy biped. Could a creature be up here following the vast caribou herds for a meal? I will never know. We did a TV story just on the track find for a local affiliate, and the original tape has not been found in my vast archive of tapes—most likely recycled, as we often did. There was no value then on such a story. Regrets forever. I somehow had not known I would make a career out of such cryptozoology mysteries. I got home and wanted answers and was stunned by the lack of resources that I could find on the topic. It was all I could think about, those tracks.

MQ: How did you conceive of the show, *Monster Quest*, and what do you think its greatest findings were?

DH: I spent the next decade focusing on other science research, on other wildlife mysteries surroundings bears, beavers, and underwater mysteries using cameras and the internet to share my findings. Finally, in my search, I came across the BFRO about 1999, and Matt Moneymaker filled me in on a laundry list of simple facts on sasquatches. I wondered why these facts and others that could surely be discovered were not common knowledge. It was then my goal to produce a science doc on the topic.

Two years after being turned down on my own, a couple of TV

agents took on the task to represent me, and *Sasquatch: Legend Meets Science* was sold to Discovery Channel. It was a landmark film. It wasn't long after that, I was asked to produce the first TV series ever on the Bigfoot mystery. *Mysterious Encounters* was born and ran for only one season and was cancelled only because the network decided to just produce live sporting events. *Mysterious Encounters* was packed with high tech, using thermal cams, drones and helium balloons, camera traps, and even the backpack—dual-record backpacks were designed and built by me as a way to film a Bigfoot encounter in the dark, but also a way to capture the reaction in real time of the witness, all using IR tech. These backpacks did work well and were then copied and used in the *Finding Bigfoot* series many years later and in a spinoff UFO series hosted by James Fox.

IR tech was brand new then, and I was lucky to be the first person to apply it on national TV for wildlife research, etcetera. *The Man who Walks with Bears*— I devised these small-footprint camera traps myself with just the record head showing and the recording devices and power buried or placed from the camera head up to a hundred feet. No commercial trail cams were available yet. My camera traps actually were much smaller and less visible than the ones now that are so common and just strapped to a tree. My traps could be hidden better and in more creative ways.

Then, I started to pitch a series on Giganto, and the pitch went nowhere, until one day, I added the tagline, "Giganto: the Real King Kong." My goal was to date Giganto teeth properly and go to China to hunt for new fossils plus put out the theory that Bigfoot may be a relative, a living Giganto, and only interview law enforcement folks as witnesses. Hunting for fossils in China and living specimens in Washington. The show was sold to History Channel, and as I produced it, I knew it was going to be an amazing show. It was everything almost that I had hoped for when it aired. The next day, when the ratings came in, I received a call asking if I could produce more of these shows in the same style and, using the same amount of science, apply it to other cryptid topics. I said yes, and *MonsterQuest* was born. It was a huge hit TV series, and I went on to produce these for four more years. I produced double seasons. It was a passion-filled, massive undertaking but highly successful. The series roughly ended in 2009–2010.

MQ: *Monster Quest* sometimes received ribbing for never actually finding the creatures it searched for, but that wasn't entirely accurate, as there were occasional successes. What would you say were the best ones?

DH: During the filming of the series, we had a number of firsts and finds. First true giant squid filmed, and was the first confirmed Architeuthis dux filmed alive in its natural habitat at great depth. First massive shark filmed inland in fresh water, a twelve-foot Greenland shark. Biggest croc filmed. New tech developed laser-measuring lens. Biggest Komodo dragon filmed. Modern well-equipped expedition to the Himalayan mountains for the yeti. Possibly the first DNA of a bigfoot to show a possible chimpanzee connection. First to attach cameras to many wild animals. Cut the path for many Bigfoot shows to follow.

[Author's note: To this, I would add rocks being thrown at Bigfoot researchers on more than one occasion, a trail cam photo possibly showing the back of a live (though officially extinct) thylacine, or Tasmanian tiger, and a scary close encounter between a scuba diver and what may have been Ogopogo, the monster of Okanagan Lake in British Columbia.]

MQ: *Monster Quest* covered a case in season three from Staples, Minnesota, in which a female witness struck a large, upright, hairy creature, which the show depicted as being a bigfoot, with her car, and then two young men shot at the creature. I have heard investigators of that case state that what the witnesses described was more like a "dogman" or werewolf-type creature than a bigfoot. What do you think was the true nature of that case?

DH: Do not know what to conclude. We did our best to solve it.

MQ: How would you rate Minnesota as a "Bigfoot state" compared to other regions more commonly associated with the creatures such as the Pacific Northwest?

DH: Minnesota has all the elements as the PNW with the exception of mild winters. Bigfoot in Minnesota stays clear of our prairie areas and sticks to our forest areas near water and, when present, hills, like along the St. Croix River and the Iron Range. People in Minnesota are far less likely to report a sighting than the PNW.

MQ: You produced the Discovery Channel special, *Sasquatch: Legend Meets Science* in 2003, and now twenty years later, as this book is being prepared, you are working on its sequel, *Sasquatch: Legend Meets Science 2*. What do you think the first special contributed to Bigfoot research, and what do you hope to further accomplish with the second?

DH: It raised the bar a bit, showing science can be applied to the mystery. *Legend Meets Science 2* will raise that same bar a bit higher. I have no doubt.

MQ: What prompted you to want to expand into the publishing world with your company Hangar 1 Publishing, in addition to your work in television?

DH: I wanted to give an opportunity to new writers or writers that didn't know how to approach the publishing world. With our IBT technology integration, it's also a major change to the publishing world. It allows video and audio in both print books and e-books. An example of a book that fits IBT so well is the *Freeman Bigfoot Files* book, as we wanted to include Paul Freeman's audio diary he recorded over many years and some of the footage he shot. Another project that comes to mind is *Unknown Sounds* by David Ellis. That will utilize IBT tech to the max.

MQ: You've been involved with the Randy Bauer case near Black-duck, Minnesota, the subject of my 2021 book, which you published, *Sasquatch Central*. This case has repeated Bigfoot activity intertwined with what seems to be various paranormal phenomena. With your experience, what is your opinion on whether Bigfoot is just a natural flesh and blood creature or if there might be some paranormal element to it?

DH: I have no solid conclusion on what a sasquatch may be, except this: Bigfoot needs to be studied scientifically, and concluding they have paranormal connections is no excuse for ignoring collecting evidence on all levels.

MQ: What do you think is being done right in the Bigfoot field at the present time, and what do you think is being done wrong?

DH: Easier to say what's being done wrong generally. Most researchers do not collect evidence or even try to, yet evidence analysis is getting cheaper, such as DNA. Also, very little fresh ideas are tried in that evidence collection. Finally, GIS mapping and data input is finally being done on a large scale by a couple of individuals.

MQ: You've been fortunate in being able to apply some considerable personal financial wealth to the field of Bigfoot research, and some might compare you to the late Texas oilman, Tom Slick, who did the same thing back in the early days of Bigfooting in the 1950s Pacific Northwest and also in the search for the yeti in the Himalayas. What do you think of that comparison, and would you ever consider doing as Slick did and funding people to be in the field full time searching for Bigfoot?

DH: As a general rule, I just finance my own research, both lab and field. However, field efforts have had my help where new tech was the plan to be implemented. As example, I helped Adam Colt's thirty-day solo field effort with gear and tech.

MQ: Any final thoughts you might have are welcome.

DH: In the world of Bigfoot, the rules of the sightings are clear. Anywhere woods, water, and hills are available, there is a chance—at least a chance—that a sasquatch passes through the area. It is a very geographic-specific problem and mystery. This mystery is never going away, ever, as it's fueled every week by numerous sightings by credible people, so to ignore this mystery is a true tragedy of modern times.

BRIAN GLYNN

Like Doug Hajicek, I met Brian Glynn through my involvement in the Randy Bauer case near Black-duck, which has drawn so many researchers and interested people to visit the property and try to learn what they can. A resident of Bemidji, which is only a half hour drive from the property, Brian has been a regular there and enjoys staking out the place, sitting in deer stands, watching and listening for long periods of time, and just waiting for whatever might happen. When I met him, I realized that I had already written about him in my 2019 book, *Bigfoot Chronicle*, as he had had encounters with Bigfoot prior to ever visiting the Bauer property, and once he did, there would be more to come.

Brian responded to a list of questions for this book in July 2023:

MIKE QUAST: Can you give a brief background on yourself, what you do for a living, etcetera?

BRIAN GLYNN: I just retired June 2 of this year after thirty years as a school psychologist. I've been spending summers working at the Bemidji Town & Country Club as a maintenance person, and I mow everything on the course. I grew up in the town of Staples, which is in north-central Minnesota, then spent seven years working for Burlington Northern Railroad before graduating college at Concordia College in Moorhead and getting my master's in specialist degrees at Moorhead State University.

MQ: How did you first get involved with the subject of Bigfoot, and can you relate some of the most interesting experiences you've had with it?

BG: I've always been interested in the cryptid world and have a very open mind about some of the possibilities. I've only seen a UFO one time and can actually verify seeing a bigfoot one time, but I've had several experiences that suggest to me that I've had experience with Bigfoot. One such experience was in a summer evening after dark. I remembered that I had left the garden sprinkler on, so I went outside, crossed the deck, then went to the side of the house to turn the tap off. As I was walking towards the tap, about five feet away from me, I heard a low, guttural growl. Most people's first instinct at that moment would be to freeze or turn and run, but I stopped and had a very calm feeling come over me, and said out loud, "Stop your growling. I'm just gonna turn the sprinkler off." The whole feeling was one of calmness, euphoria, and peace. I turned my back to the source of the growl, which was very odd, then walked back into the house. About a half hour later, I was sitting in my chair, when I had this sudden realization that something weird just happened to me and went outside to look but didn't see anything. The weird part was that I was in a very calm and peaceful spot, and I feel that I had experienced infrasound. I've often considered that what I experienced may be what deer and other prey animals experience when Bigfoot is near and use infrasound, and that I would've done absolutely anything at that point.

The Bigfoot I saw at Randy's place was probably only fifteen feet away from me and walked calmly across the trail in front of me, and I then stopped where it crossed to see if I could see any tracks or smell anything, but I could not. I then sat by the campfire for an hour, very quiet and feeling odd, before I realized what I had seen. Again, I think somehow, either by Bigfoot or my internal mechanisms, I was kind of out of it. I've also been at Randy's place when we took a picture, and there was a hairy hand in front of our picture, but we could not see anything in front of us as that point. I became nauseous and disoriented and dizzy, and I think at that point, being in such close proximity either affected me via infrasound or—just being that close, even though I couldn't see them. I've also had a number of very strong smells at Randy's place when others right next to me couldn't smell a thing. One night, I was by the campfire by myself, when I got up to take a leak, and as I was standing there. It was a very strong odor of Bigfoot, but I could not see anything next to me. I wonder if they can cloak physically only.

Perhaps the oddest incident at Randy's place was, one evening, I was sitting alone in a deer stand when I heard young children's voices, laughing and playing in the woods, and when I asked Randy later about the neighbors that direction, he said nobody lived in that direction for five miles. Shortly after the noises in the woods, though, I had a crow circle my tree around and around with its head turned looking at me the entire time. That is very odd behavior for a crow to be that close to humans. Later, then I got cold, so I got down to walk back towards the house, and when I got near the house, I could hear Randy and others he was with yelling at me as they thought I was still in that stand. Randy swears that there was somebody in that tree when I was not. Seemed like a time glitch.

[Author's note: Randy instead thinks that after Brian left the tree stand, a small Bigfoot climbed up into it, and that is what he and the others saw and mistakenly thought was Brian still there.]

So far, I am the only person that has ever spent an entire night in Randy's woods all my myself. I did that one night last summer when I got into a tree stand at 3 PM and left the next morning at 6 AM. During that night though, I heard an odd noise very close to me, but in the deep trees, so I couldn't see anything. It was sort of a clicking type of sound. Right after that experience, I started having premonitions of things about to happen. Very, very clear premonitions of upcoming events, even though the events were very minor. It was not like I could predict a plane crash or something like that. The first one was when I was at a gas station, and it jumped into my head that the lady next to me was going to drive off with a nozzle still in her tank, and she did just that. The next one was where I was mowing my yard, and I had a flash in my head that the mower tire was going to come off, and it did just that. It's hard to explain, but these feelings were extremely vivid and like I've never had before. They've stopped though, and I don't know why. I do hear other researchers talk about getting paranormal strengths after having encounters with cryptids, extraterrestrials, UFOs, or other types of paranormal activity.

MQ: Do you consider yourself a Bigfoot researcher, or more like just an ordinary individual whose experiences have led you to want to take part in the field?

BG: I'm not sure I would consider myself a researcher, but I am very interested in the phenomenon. I've also had a number of incidences over my lifetime that suggest I may have the ability to be attuned to odd stuff.

MQ: I know you from having met you at the Randy Bauer property near Blackduck, where Bigfoot activity has been ongoing. Would you consider that case to be the most intense that you've seen?

BG: For the last sixteen years, I've worked at the Bemidji Town & Country Club mowing fairways, greens, etcetera, so I have a lot of time listening to podcasts and audio books. I've heard a lot of podcasts talking about Bigfoot and other cryptid activities, and I think Randy's area ranks right up there with the most intense areas. I'm not sure why certain location are hotbeds of activity, but I suspect it has something to do with interdimensional portals or something along that line. Part of the reason I say this is that animals the size of the one I saw and other big ones in Randy's immediate area do not have enough food to sustain themselves. An 800-pound would need to eat a deer every other day, and there's just not that many in that area or any area; therefore, I think they travel to other dimensions or other realities where they get sustenance.

MQ: With your experiences, do you have an opinion on whether you think Bigfoot is a flesh and blood animal or if you think there might be some paranormal element involved?

BG: I strongly believe that Bigfoot are from another dimension or another reality. There's just been too much evidence of Bigfoot encounters where they simply disappear into thin air, like, several times at Randy's place, or there's been orbs, like at Randy's place, or there's UFO activity in the same area. I also don't think that a small territory would have enough food for them to survive.

MQ: Do you have an end goal in mind for yourself in the search for Bigfoot?

BG: Probably be my most two pressing goals are, one, to have another sighting, and, two, to have interactions like I had that one night where I was given paranormal strengths, even though they didn't last very long.

ADRIAN LEE

Though I was not able to secure an interview with Adrian Lee, I was encouraged to include him in this book, as he has brought a strong scholarly approach to Bigfoot research in Minnesota. Adrian hails from Great Britain, growing up in London, and has a rich history as a researcher, teacher, author, musician, and producer of videos, radio shows, and podcasts. He is the founder of the International Paranormal Society and a member of the Luton Paranormal Society in England, and he's been investigating urban legends, ghosts and hauntings, and a myriad of other paranormal subjects for well over twenty-five years.

When called to come to the United States, Adrian came to Minnesota in 2008, where he has lived ever since, living in Minneapolis where he spent two years as the international correspondent for a live paranormal talk radio show, as well as living in

Sauk Centre in the St. Cloud metro area and Windom in the southwest part of the state. A very prolific author, his books include *Mysterious Midwest, Mysterious Minnesota, How to be a Christian Psychic*, and *Ghosts & UFOs: Connecting Paranormal Phenomena Through Quantum Physics*, among many others. He is a widespread and popular lecturer and also skilled as a psychic, clairvoyant, reiki healer, and tarot reader.

I've met Adrian, as he was a fellow presenter when I was invited to speak about Bigfoot at the 2022 ValleyCon sci-fi and fantasy convention in Fargo, North Dakota, and in having his table right next to mine, I came to learn what a wonderful charismatic sense of humor he has, delivered, of course, with his classic British accent. We were both selling books, and he sold way more than me.

Once entrenched into paranormal research in Minnesota, Adrian has taken an interest in Bigfoot and has been involved in looking into cases in southern Minnesota where he lives, and I look forward to learning more about what he is able to uncover.

MARC RUYAK

In 2016, the small Minnesota town of Remer in the southern part of the Chippewa National Forest, which has a population of just around 400 people, declared itself the "Home of Bigfoot," making it so by launching the first annual Remer Bigfoot Days festival, which was to take place every year on the first weekend after the Fourth of July. It is a fun and celebratory time with sporting events and food vendors and things for sale all in the name of Bigfoot, but also serious Bigfoot researchers setting up booths in which they invite people to come and share their experiences, and town meetings that take place in the city center where, in addition to Bigfoot-calling contests that the children are invited to take part in, the adults are also welcome to stand up and give their accounts of encounters with Bigfoot. The event draws hundreds of visitors, bringing incredible attention to the little town, and in its first year, it was even featured on the Animal Planet TV show, *Finding Bigfoot*. It had to shut down for a spell, first due to the Covid epidemic, and then because of road construction that tore up the town's main street for several months, but after that, it came back as strong as ever. There are several likenesses of Bigfoot both large and small on display throughout the town, and a convenience store called Bigfoot Gas & Gifts that has a large Bigfoot statue for people's amusement as well as a display of a few footprint casts and other artifacts from the area, and a copy of my own book, *Bigfoot Chronicle*, which documents nearly 700 Bigfoot reports from Minnesota. (Shameless plug).

Abe DelRio of the Minnesota Bigfoot Research Team, who does particularly much research and fieldwork around the town, and Jen Kruse of the She-Squatchers, have been regular fixtures of the event, serving as kind of masters of ceremony, but the original brainchild of Remer Bigfoot Days was Marc Ruyak, a local business owner and school board authority who first came up with the idea for the festival and continues to be the organizer of this event that brings so much attention to the subject of Bigfoot in Minnesota. He responded to a recorded interview for this book during the festival on July 6, 2024.

MIKE QUAST: For a first question, can I just ask your age and occupation?

MARC RUYAK: Sure. I'm self-employed, I own a small excavating business, and I'm fifty-six years old.

MQ: You're the creator and organizer of the annual Remer Bigfoot Days festival. Can you describe how you came up with the idea and then brought it to life, and why you feel that, out of all the small towns in the Chippewa National Forest area, Remer is the one that should be known as the Home of Bigfoot?

MR: So, it started back in 2009, when there was trail camera picture that ended up being a hoax, but it kind of spurred interest in me to start doing some research about Bigfoot sightings in the area. So I talked to several of the research teams and began to find out that there was a lot of activity in and around the area of Remer and specifically within five, six, seven miles of Remer, and I started looking at historical data and even found a lot of stuff that was decades old, of sightings and stuff. So I thought, in my own mind, this is the Home of Bigfoot, and I began to pursue trademarking Remer as the Home of Bigfoot, and as I talked to researchers, we even had the TV show, *Finding Bigfoot*, out here, and they agreed that Remer was the Home of Bigfoot. And the amount of sightings and the amount of activity around here is just far greater than any other area in recent times.

MQ: Have you had experiences yourself in which you thought you were in close proximity to Bigfoot?

MR: I have not had any myself, but I know I've listened to thousands of stories, and I'm just very intrigued, and some I can't explain —the stories around here. So, I'm very intrigued and hopeful someday that I do have a close encounter or a sighting myself.

MQ: What is it that motivates you in your involvement with the Bigfoot phenomenon, and do you have an end goal in mind?

MR: Probably the biggest thing in my mind is, when I started doing my research, I was upset with the fact that when people had a story or a sighting about Bigfoot they were ridiculed, and that really bothered me, because it's not up to other people to judge whether or not something is true and whether or not somebody saw something.

That's up to that person. They know it to be true, and there were so many people that I talked to that didn't want to tell their story, because of that ridicule. And so, my biggest thing and my end goal for doing this in our area was to let people know that there's no shame or harm in telling your story, and to take the stigma away from being a storyteller of Bigfoot. And if you have a sighting or an experience or something that you can't explain, I wanted Remer to be the home where you can come and tell your story about Bigfoot, tell about your experience, talk about things that you can't explain that you've seen in the woods and feel comfortable to be able to do that. Remer is that place, where you can come tell any of your Bigfoot stories, and we want to hear them. And that's really the end goal—is to take the stigma away and take the shame away and have Remer as a place where you can feel comfortable to come and tell your story about Bigfoot.

MQ: Okay, last question. With your experience, what is your opinion on whether Bigfoot is a flesh and blood animal or if there might be some kind of paranormal element involved?

MR: I'm always intrigued, and in fact, this year is probably more so than normal. I've heard some stories that I never heard before, and it's caused me to think in different ways about Bigfoot. In years past, I hadn't heard that many stories about the paranormal activity, and I'm hearing more and more about them. And some of them seem to make sense, and some of them seem to be explanations for why there aren't different things happening with regard to evidence and tracks and other things, so I'm open to anything, and I want to hear more stories, because I think the best way to explain things is by more information, not less. So, I want those stories to come out. I want those people who think things or have researched things to talk about them, because the best way to find out about stuff is more information, not less. And so, hopefully, the more of those experiences people have, and ideas and research, the more they come to Remer and talk about those things and bring those out, because someday maybe we'll have an explanation if we keep talking about these things.

RANDY BAUER

The man, the legend, Randy Bauer, and the Bigfoot activity on his property near Blackduck, Minnesota were the focus of my 2021 book, *Sasquatch Central: High Strangeness at a Northern Minnesota Homestead*. Since the activity began, he has become one of the most important and sought-out figures in Minnesota Bigfoot research, and a majority of the investigators featured in this current book have visited his property at one time or another. In his mid-sixties, he is a musician who plays saxophone and keyboards as frontman of a boogie-woogie swing band called Smokehouse, a sound engineer with his own production company that works with many other bands around the country, an avid outdoorsman and hunter, a prolific family man and patriarch, and now a Bigfoot researcher himself, with a Facebook group simply titled "Randy's Bigfoot Research" that chronicles his journey in dealing with the creatures that dwell around his home. It is a major habituation case, a term for the rare occurrences in which someone has repeated activity going on for an extended time, during which they seem to be able to develop a trust and rapport with Bigfoot creatures. It is also a case that has brought to the forefront the possibility that Bigfoot is not just a flesh and blood animal but a kind of paranormal entity, something that I had resisted for many years until having no choice to confront it when I discovered Randy's case.

Randy is clear in explaining that before the activity began around his home, he had absolutely no opinion on Bigfoot and that whether it existed or not wasn't something he had ever even thought about. Today, however, he is adamant in his assertion that the creatures are very real but that they are not a natural part of this world, and he has decided to become a strong spokesman for that position. The following chapter contains a major update in the ongoing story of the activity around his home, but for this chapter, he provided a statement on April 22, 2024.

"There are want-to-be-believers, meaning they want to believe, but they've never seen anything. There are believers—they have seen one. And there are knowers, who have interaction with them all the time. I'm a knower.

"This all started for me in 2013. Sasquatch was never on my mind. When I started to see evidence from them, I, like a lot of people, thought they were just a big animal hiding in the woods, but now I know different. They are not an animal hiding behind a tree, and you don't see them. They are a people; they have families. Here's what I do know for sure. I know what they are not. They are interdimensional. They do not live on our Earth as we know. They do not live in caves. They do not go back in swamps when it's forty below in Minnesota to get warm. But they do come to our Earth a lot. They do go in caves and swamps. This is what they have told me in mindspeak. I've seen sasquatch a lot and close up, in the day time, in the open. We look at each other. One more thing I do— I'm not trying to get evidence for the world. I don't do cameras, whoops, knocks. I am interacting with them, and they are with me. They trust me. I will talk to anyone and teach them what I know, but they have to be willing to take it seriously. bauerrandy1@gmail.com.

This is not opinion. These are my experiences.

7

"SASQUATCH CENTRAL" UPDATE

Much of Bigfooting is done in state or national forest areas, where one does not need permission to go and has free reign to explore at will. Only twice in my life have I been privileged to be granted access to privately owned land on which Bigfoot activity was occurring. The first was in the early 1990s, in Clearwater County, Minnesota, when an elderly retired tracker and trapper named Ed Trimble was finding strange bipedal tracks and hearing mysterious howls on his property and having the beehives that he kept broken into by something that, unlike bears, which he was very familiar with, did not leave teeth or claw marks. Ed never had any actual sightings of what was haunting his land, but he introduced me to several of his neighbors who had had sightings of typical looking Bigfoot creatures, and it was while camping on his property in my early twenties that I had my first ever experience of hearing what I believe to have been Bigfoot vocalizations, crazy high-pitched screams that I was absolutely not ready for.

Ed became a bit of a mentor to me back then in my younger days, teaching me a lot about being out in the wilderness, and I affectionately called him the "old man of the woods," chronicling his story in my early self-published books. He eventually passed away, and I miss him to this day.

My second opportunity to have access to private land came at the tail end of 2019, when I heard about a property near the town of Blackduck in Beltrami County where Bigfoot activity was said to have been going on continuously since late 2013. When I contacted the landowner, Randy Bauer, he made himself very available, as he was actively engaged in working with any interested Bigfoot researchers in an attempt to understand what was going on all around him, so, for a second time, I became friends with someone who had a continuous Bigfoot episode going on. This one, however, was by far more intense than Ed Trimble's case, and in fact, it would become the most exciting and most documented case I have ever encountered and would become the focus of my 2021 book, *Sasquatch Central: High Strangeness at a Northern Minnesota Homestead* during the time when Doug Hajicek, of television's *Monster Quest* fame, got interested in entering the publishing field and offered to have all of my previously self-published books done up in professional form.

Randy Bauer is in his sixties and is a musician by trade, leading a boogie-woogie swing band called Smokehouse and also doing sound engineering for other bands across the country. In his spare time, he loves to spend time in the wilderness that surrounds his home—an avid hunter and explorer of the woods. It was during a period spanning 2013–2014 that he began to find evidence of a mysterious and frightening presence around his home that would eventually evolve into a dramatic and extensive investigation that turned out to involve not only Bigfoot but also a seemingly paranormal element. It is a habituation case, one in which a person develops a relationship with Bigfoot creatures over time through various types of interaction, such as exchanging of gifts, and I had often seen warnings within the Bigfoot field to steer clear of habituation cases. Skeptical researchers would say that Bigfoot experiences were so extremely rare, that anyone who claimed to have them repeatedly was bound to be a hoaxer, and especially if they claimed any kind of supernatural trait. But after I got to know Randy, I became convinced that he was absolutely not a hoaxer and that he was being 100% honest in his claims. He has now a few years of history of leaving jar after jar of peanut butter out in the woods as offerings, and the creatures responding by taking this bait in ways that show that they have the dexterity and intelligence to unscrew and then replace the lids on these jars with big and deep finger marks left in the peanut butter. Sometimes, they also take the jars away but leave the lids on the ground, arranged by color with all the red ones together, all the blue ones together, etc.

Randy's case is a treasure trove of activity. It involves multiple sightings of creatures by multiple witnesses, family members, neighbors, and visiting researchers, including huge ones said to be up to ten feet tall. It has the usual tracks being found and plaster casts being made, and a wide range of stick structures have been found in the surrounding woods that do not seem to be natural formations— large teepee- or pyramid-type structures, and depictions of X, A, or V shapes fashioned out of tree branches. In describing these, I always feel the need to say that I absolutely don't think it means that Bigfoot understands our alphabet, only that these are basic shapes that just happen to resemble those letters. There are deer kills that happen on and around the property that are unlike kills by any known natural predator such as bears, wolves, or mountain lions, which tear their prey apart and leave a gruesome scene. What Randy finds are sites where deer have been killed but where all that is left is a large expanse of hair on the ground over several yards, no bones or flesh remaining. And over the months and years, he has found dozens of these kill sites. He has also found dozens of deer skulls, decapitated heads that he sometimes just comes across while walking in the woods, but at other times they are found in places like the various deer stands he has around his property or even on the front porch of his house as if left as gifts for him.

Some of the most dramatic activity on Randy's property, apart from the actual sightings, are the sounds that have been heard by multiple people, including myself. Recording devices that Randy has placed in the woods have captured several typical Bigfoot screams and howls, and what is known as "samurai chatter" has also been heard by Randy and his wife right outside their bedroom window at night. It's a jabbering sound that vaguely resembles some kind of Asian language and was popularized by a famous sound recording from the early 1970s called the Sierra Sounds in California. Randy also likens it to the babblings of the Tasmanian Devil from the Loony Tunes cartoons. I, myself, have heard sounds while camping on Randy's property that sound like indistinct human voices calling out when it's known that there is no one out there. There have even been photographs captured by trail cameras on the property that, although falling short of final proof, seem to show the creatures in various phases of trying to stay out of frame, as if they recognize cameras as an unwelcome annoyance.

In addition to the standard Bigfoot activity, a paranormal or supernatural element is strongly involved with this case. One of the first experiences Randy had was finding huge bipedal footprints in snow that just ended in the middle of a clearing, as if the track maker had simply vanished. There has been actual poltergeist-type activity inside Randy's house. Floating orbs of light have frequently been seen, and some stories of such things that seem to defy the limits of the imagination, such as a sighting by Randy and another man of a glowing portal in the dark of night, from which two large orbs of light emerged and then morphed into Bigfoot creatures. The question of whether Bigfoot is a natural flesh and blood animal or might have a paranormal or supernatural element to it really comes to a head at Randy's place. I have always been on the fence about such things, but this case has made me strongly consider whether there might be some kind of paranormal energy out in the woods that Bigfoot is smart enough to detect and interact with, or if Bigfoot itself might be a paranormal entity. Clearly, they possess a physical aspect, as Randy has collected numerous hair samples he believes they leave behind. He suspects they frequent areas like the powerline corridor running through his property, using the poles to scratch their backs.

Some of these samples have been analyzed by Doug Hajicek, who says they match past samples from other cases that have been concluded to be Bigfoot hair. At this time, much more in-depth research is slated to be done on this, but for now, I am going to give an account of all activity that has gone on on Randy's property since the publication of my book, *Sasquatch Central*.

The book concludes by noting that there could be no satisfying ending, since the story is bound to continue. It instead features a brief description of my final visit there on Saturday, December 12, 2020. It seems fitting now to begin this update by revisiting that day, because a closer look at what transpired ended up adding much to the overall mystery of the place.

That afternoon, Randy, his stepson Tanner, who lives with him, John Badger of the SRA, and myself went on a hike out to an area of state-owned land that lies close to Randy's property. Randy wanted to show us a cedar swamp just beyond a river that he thought was an area of interest. Just minutes after departing the house, we found what we took to be a few medium-size Bigfoot tracks in the shallow, patchy snow, a tantalizing find that made us excited for what might be to come. After making our way to the state land, we came to a huge teepee-shaped stick structure, the largest Randy had ever found, and I was at first very excited over it and thought it was new, until Randy reminded me that I had already seen this one on a previous visit, and I had to admit how lost I would still feel navigating these woods without his guidance. About fifty yards from this teepee was a stand of pine trees and a barbed wire fence line we had just crossed. This will become important a little later in this anecdote.

Continuing on from the teepee, we headed north toward the river and the cedar swamp for several arduous minutes and along the way came across two odd, rectangular holes in the ground. They were definitely not natural occurrences, but Randy couldn't fathom who might have made them, as hardly anyone ever came out to this area. After briefly examining them, he asked if we still wanted to keep going, and we all said yes, so on we went, ever north, with Randy beginning to outdistance us, as he is known to do, until he got a 100 yards ahead, at which point, he called out to us about something he had just found. When we caught up to him, he was excitedly examining another huge teepee structure, one he said had not been there before. We spent considerable time in this spot taking pictures and video, and I even posed for some shots sitting inside the teepee. Randy then pointed out that it was nearly 4:30 and that if we still wanted to go on and see the cedar swamp, it would be dark before we'd get back to the house, so we cut the hike short and headed back toward the south. After we returned to the first big teepee structure, we continued to Randy's property and then to his house, where we visited for a bit before saying our goodbyes for the evening and going our separate ways.

This visit, fairly mundane for Randy's place, grew more significant as Randy studied the photos and video we'd taken. The further he examined them, the stranger things became. In the pictures of the second teepee structure, in the background, he could clearly see the pine trees and fence line present at the first teepee structure. Slowly, it dawned on him: there was no second teepee. We had somehow been back at the first not realizing it was the same one. How, then, had we been able to reverse direction from what we thought was the second and come back to the first yet again on our way back to the house without realizing anything was amiss? Mystified, in the days that followed, Randy went back out to examine our tracks in the snow. Surely, he thought, we must have somehow gotten disoriented and been walking in circles. But no, our tracks went absolutely straight north from the first teepee to a spot where there now was no second teepee, and then straight back south to the first one again. To say that it made no sense was an understatement. It was an absolute mind bender.

The place was already well known for paranormal goings on, effects on electronics and perhaps even on people's bodies and minds, and in trying to rationalize this event, it seems impossible to explain in any kind of natural way. We all know what we saw that day, and it is documented on film, yet the tracks in the snow make it impossible. I couldn't help but think, based on things seen by Randy and John, of the alleged glowing dimensional portals in this place, through which the Bigfoot creatures were believed to travel—things postulated about in quantum physics but never proven and not understood by most laymen. The one time when the men had seen such a portal was at night, and I wondered if such a thing would still be visible if it appeared in the light of day. If not, and if one out walking in the woods happened to just blunder into it because it was invisible, what would happen? What would it feel like? Was it possible that it wouldn't feel like anything, and that if shaken up and downright teleported by something like that, one might not even realize that it had happened? I know how crazy that sounds, and that it is all just pure speculation, but after this experience, I really don't know what else to think. There was no spot where our tracks in the snow just ended and then began again somewhere else. Randy has speculated about an image of the first teepee somehow being projected onto the spot where we thought the second one was, but it was absolutely no hologram, because we were touching it, and it was solid. This is truly a mystery for the ages.

In March of 2021, Randy left a trail camera facing where he had placed some venison on the ground in the state land as bait. The meat was taken, and the camera captured a clear photo of what looked like a dark, hairy hand at the bottom of the frame with fingers and even nails clearly visible. This happened as my book, *Sasquatch Central*, was being prepared for professional publication, and I was asked to add an addendum to it to include this potentially important incident, which I did. Doug Hajicek would ask Randy to try and duplicate the shot, and he had some difficulty figuring out how a creature could have been down low on the ground and gotten its hand into that exact position, but eventually, he found that the only way it worked was if the creature was behind the tree holding the camera, not in front of it, and was reaching around it. Much was made of the similarity in appearance between this hand and that of a chimpanzee.

In April, Randy hiked out to the same area where the hand photo had been taken and along the way happened to find a deflated party balloon on the ground, apparently having drifted away from someone's birthday party somewhere and fallen to earth here in the middle of the woods. He picked it up and tied it to a tree. Four days later, he found that it was untied and back on the ground, so he tied it up again. Shortly thereafter, he returned to the site again with Tanner and Bigfoot witness and enthusiast Brian Glynn to do the attempted reconstruction at the hand site, requested by Doug Hajicek, and on their way in, they found that the balloon was gone. While doing their work at the hand site, Brian suddenly felt extremely ill. It only lasted a short time and has been suggested to be an effect of infrasound, a low-frequency ability that is known to be used by some predators to stun and incapacitate their prey, and which Bigfoot is thought by some to employ. At the same time, the camera still up at that site captured something huge and dark lurking at the extreme right of the frame just a few feet from where the men were standing, yet they saw nothing there at the time. Several such photos have been captured in this case, the kind that suggests much but proves little to nothing. On their hike out, the men found that a broken poplar tree that had not been there before had been lain across the trail.

The next day, Randy and Tanner went back to the hand site and decided to just sit quietly for a while on some logs about ten feet apart, sort of a form of meditation and just trying to tap into the flow of the wind and whatever other energy might be flowing through the woods. After a few minutes, something most unexpected happened. A violent blow of some kind suddenly knocked Randy off of his log, but again, there was nothing visible to account for it. A loud whistling then came out of the woods that repeated seven times, seeming to answer back when Randy whistled in response to it.

A final thing that happened in April was that while out walking in the woods, Randy happened upon a deer skull, that of a small buck, the head had been pressed down and sunken into the ground with just the antlers protruding. Through those antlers, two broken birch branches had been placed, forming an X. He had found so many deer skulls over the years, some by happenstance and others that seemed to have been left in places deliberately for him to find, and it was always strange that there were no other remains around except for these severed heads. This particular find, though, has to rank as one of the most bizarre ever, as there was no doubt that it absolutely could not have occurred naturally.

Birch branches placed in an X between deer antlers pressed into the ground.

These occurrences were intriguing but did not offer a look at what was behind them. Actual creature sightings have hardly been a stranger to Randy's case, though, and one occurred during the weekend that spanned the end of April and beginning of May 2021, when members of the SRA were visiting, as they have done a handful of times. Todd Newby, John Badger, and a member named Mike were present, as well as myself. I recall well that I went during an afternoon out to a spot on Randy's forty acres, where I had previously conducted an experiment in which I'd placed mirrors in trees with a camera facing them to try and entice the creatures to come and investigate and possibly get their pictures taken.

This had ended badly, with all the mirrors thrown to the ground, one of them shattered, and my camera turned sideways on its tree with mud smeared all over it, and, of course, no pictures captured of what had done it. On this day, when I went to casually check out that site again, I found something that has been a recurring element of Randy's story hanging from the tree that had held the camera: a "Y stick," or simply, a small tree limb in the shape of the letter Y that Randy believes the creatures sometimes leave as gifts or cryptic messages. It did not seem to have just fallen there naturally, but I had no idea as to its meaning. I was just excited to feel that it had been left at what I kind of considered to be my own personal site on the property, and I took it down and have it as a keepsake to this day.

That night, as everyone was sitting around Randy's campfire area, where much Bigfoot activity has occurred, John and Mike decided to venture out on a nocturnal walk along the fence lines that mark the boundary between Randy's land and cow pastures owned by a neighbor. As he described in his interview earlier in this book, John suddenly saw something astonishing. A huge upright bipedal silhouette broke out of some trees in the pasture, ran fast toward the fence ahead, vaulted over it like an athlete, then disappeared back into the woods on the other side without making a sound. Mike was a bit behind John and missed out on seeing this. When they got back to the campfire, they told the rest of us of the sighting, astonishing us all and making us wish we had gone with them on their walk. To pin down the size of the figure, I asked John if he thought it was big enough to be the ten-foot creature Randy had seen, and he said yes.

Within the next couple of days, John showed Randy the exact spot of the sighting, and they established the GPS coordinates of it, which they also shared with Doug Hajicek when they related the story to him. Randy went out by himself to check it out on an afternoon and didn't find any tracks but did locate a deer bone tucked into a cleft in a tree in the area the creature had run into. Then something unexpected happened. While he was exploring the spot, an extremely low flying airplane suddenly appeared, so low that Randy could see the pilot and clearly read the markings on the side of the plane. He waved to the pilot but got no response as he watched the plane circle the site eight times before finally flying away. This incident gave Randy enough information to research it, and he found that the plane had been chartered from the airport in the city of Bemidji, a half hour drive away, and that its flight plan was to travel straight to that spot and then right back again, but the identity of the customer was confidential.

There will be those who call it conspiracy theory that some mysterious human entity out there might have taken an interest in Randy's case and is surveilling the property, but this incident simply is what it is. Randy briefly wondered if the plane might have been hired by Doug Hajicek to do some filming for future documentaries, but the two of them are friends, and Doug assured him that was not the case. Yet, someone had gotten wind of the GPS coordinates that had been shared between the men, so something of a clandestine nature did seem to have been committed by someone. What the pilot was hoping to see is anyone's guess, since the tree canopy offers little view of the ground from above. It is the only incident of its kind within the overall story, so it stands as its own head-scratching mystery.

Shortly thereafter, Doug Hajicek's deep interest in Randy's case led him to launch a new and well-funded research project on the property. In early May, Doug's son, Adam, came to install several high-tech closed-circuit TV cameras throughout the patch of woods just behind Randy's house. This involved stringing many, many yards of cable along the ground that would be camouflaged as well as possible. The cameras themselves would be disguised to blend in with the surroundings. They were to film around the clock for several months, capturing anything and everything to pass by. Randy was reticent about it because of the relationship he believed he had achieved with the creatures and how he knew they felt about cameras, something he had started to steer away from using so as to develop further trust with them, but he agreed to the project.

On the first night the cameras were installed, something incredible happened, and the fact that it failed to be documented is maddening. I admit to being a complete novice when it comes to modern technology of this kind, so my understanding of it is limited, but on this night, Doug was at his home in the Twin Cities metro area watching a live feed of the footage from the cameras at Randy's on his home computer, when he saw three Bigfoot creatures walking single file directly in front of one of the cameras, clear as day and without doubt. They were spaced out according to their heights, which was in the six- to eight-foot range, as far as he could tell. Seeing them rocked Doug to his core and brought him to tears. Imagine the emotional blow then when he learned that, because the fine tuning of the CCTV camera array was not quite complete yet, the footage he had just watched in real time had not been recorded. I share his pain. How I would have loved to see them. Since Randy's own sightings had been of much larger creatures, nine and ten feet tall, it raised all kinds of questions about the size variations in the area. The two giants, combined with the three medium-size ones Doug saw, made for five, and little six-inch tracks once found indicated the presence of a juvenile, probably three feet tall, making a minimum of six. It could have been much more, but one must stick with the evidence.

The CCTV cameras were a fun thing to follow for a while, and they captured many tantalizing things. Normal wildlife footage was plentiful. A camera disguised as a squirrel got attacked by a hawk, an actual squirrel crawling up a tree and passing right in front of a camera looked huge right up against the lens, and what I can only conclude was a spider crawling across a lens looked for all the world like the creepy facehugger from the movie *Alien*. But there were also things that defied explanation. There were several shots of orbs and other weird light formations floating along through the woods during times when the background foliage was still, showing there was no wind. There was one amazing bit of footage of a mysterious black mist seemingly emerging out of the ground. This especially intrigued me because, when I had done my mirror experiment, my camera had captured nocturnal still shots of something darker than the night that had drifted in and blocked out all the terrain. I try to stay open minded, but I just can't call things like that anything but paranormal in nature.

On a night in July, one of the cameras captured an image of a large, black, upright figure half hidden behind a tree with orbs of light floating around it. The picture is ambiguous and not clear enough to be proof of anything, as is so often the case, but it graces the top of the page in the Facebook group that Randy maintains to keep interested people up to date on his story.

After the several months of the CCTV cameras being in place, Randy asked to have them taken down, never having been comfortable with them. Once they were gone, he said it felt like a weight had been lifted and that a certain peace had returned.

Staying within July 2021, however, there was a night when a five-year old granddaughter of Randy's named Madison was staying the night at his house. There had been a sighting the year before shared between her older sister, Bristol, and Randy, where she had been nearby but failed to see what they saw. But then, while sleeping on the living room couch, she woke in the middle of the night to see a dark, hulking figure with glowing red eyes looking through a nearby window, which would make it extremely tall with the way the house is designed. She woke the house screaming and crying, but there has always been some doubt as to whether this really happened or if it was just a young child's frightened imagination after the earlier sighting by her sister. Dealing with such young children who witness strange things has to be done gingerly, but in time, it came out in conversation with Madison that she also claimed to have seen another Bigfoot standing out on the lawn in front of the house on another night she'd been spending there and had gotten up to look out the window.

That same month, Randy's stepdaughter, Samantha Stomberg, who is the mother of Madison and Bristol, was at Randy's house by herself doing some cleaning while he was away. She had had a frightening sighting of a bigfoot in August of 2019 while driving past the property and knew full well the truth of what lurked in the surrounding woods. On this day in July, she had to go out to retrieve something from her car, and when she did, she suddenly felt mysteriously disoriented and was struck with a powerful sense of being watched. Unsettled, she hurried back into what she saw as the safety of the house, only to then have something loudly and powerfully pound on the outside of it, something that Randy had experienced there several times. In a panic, she called Randy. He was to the north, near the town of Kelliher, on his way to meet up with the SRA, who were doing an unrelated Bigfoot investigation in that area and had stopped at a roadside eatery for a bite when he received her call.

Clearly afraid, she told him what was happening, and he did his best to calm her down, telling her to go out on to the front porch and talk to the creatures, assuring them she was visiting in peace and meant them no harm. Though very reticent, she then did so as best she could, and as if in response, she heard a loud crack not far away, as if from a branch being broken. I had met and interviewed Samantha about her earlier sighting, finding her to be a woman of few words who gave the shortest possible answers to questions, clearly not interested in bringing attention to herself over her experiences or those of her children but reluctantly willing to talk about them only as much as she needed to.

There was one final episode in July, when I visited on the 17th and 18th and stayed the night. At that time, there was a white-tailed doe with a fawn that, Randy told me, was in his forty acres and acting protective. I saw her once during the day. That night after visiting with me for a bit at his campfire site, Randy left me to sit there by myself and just watch and listen. The neighbor's pasture land was nearby, and the cows were in it. As I recall, it was at around 10 PM when I began to hear them start to act extremely agitated. I couldn't see them from where I was, but they were in a wooded area moving about rapidly through the brush and loudly bellowing over and over in a way that was not normal. I grew up on a farm with cows myself, so I speak from experience. Puzzled, I got up and tried to find a position from which I might be able to see into the woods to try and deduce what was going on, but I couldn't, and as I listened, I started to hear very loud tree breaks going on. That's no cow, I thought. Something else was doing that.

I decided to take a walk around the trail system on the forty acres as the pandemonium amongst the cows continued, with the sound of it receding somewhat into the distance as I walked. But then, as I went down one particular trail, I started to hear the bellowing of a cow close behind me, seemingly too close, with where I knew the edge of the pasture to be. Had one escaped beyond the fence? Or might there be something else happening? It is easy at Randy's place to let your imagination get the best of you, and since so many witnesses had heard so many sounds over time, that seemed to suggest that the Bigfoots were able to mimic almost any animal or human vocalization. I found myself wondering if one of the creatures was following me down this trail doing an imitation of a cow bellow. That thought was cut short, however, as I reached the point where the trail I was on ended at the powerline corridor that runs through Randy's land, and right then and there, that overprotective mother deer made another appearance. As anxious as I was at that moment, it probably would have terrified me when I suddenly heard her making a bluff charge at me from out of the woods to my right, but she also made a familiar high-pitched blowing sound that deer are known to make that let me know it was not a giant apelike monster charging out of the woods at me, so it only startled me for an instant. She stopped short, just protecting her fawn, and I continued on with my walk and can only hope the two of them stayed safe that night. The sound of the agitated cows continued for about an hour and then died down toward 11 PM.

I went back to the campfire, where I stayed for some time into the night, but nothing else happened, and I eventually retired to a guest trailer-house just across the front yard from Randy's house, where I would be sleeping. Since creature activity was not limited to the woods but sometimes happened right around the house and other buildings, this trailer was an excellent place to stake out the yard and watch out the windows at night. Some time after midnight, as I was doing that, I suddenly heard a strange sound coming from the woods directly behind Randy's house. It was subtle at first, and I wasn't sure what I was hearing, but as it continued to repeat, I honed in on a very deep voice going, "Unh, unh." Those two syllables, just two, over and over, with different periods of time in between, ranging from twenty or thirty seconds to a minute or so, but always just two. "Unh, unh." I was fascinated. It was far from being the first vocalization I'd heard at Randy's by this point, but it was different from anything I'd heard before. After several minutes of listening, I went to the trailer door and leaned my head out, and the sound still continued. Finally, I went completely outside and walked several feet into the yard, at which point, the sound stopped. I stood there and threw up my arms in frustration, thinking, well, what now? I knew that if I walked over to the spot it had been coming from, I wouldn't see anything. I found that, at this stage, I wasn't afraid of approaching the creatures, but I couldn't expect them to let me. Only later did I kick myself for never thinking to reach for my smart phone to record the sounds.

The next major incident came at the end of August, when Randy was mowing his lawn with a John Deere 425 riding mower. After working for a bit, he took a break and went inside the house to make a sandwich, leaving the mower parked close by facing in an east-west direction. When he finished his snack, he was surprised to come back outside and find that the mower was now sixty yards away from where he'd left it and facing north-south. He had not heard the sound of it starting up. That was impossible anyway, because he'd taken the key out of it, and as it had power steering, it was impossible to push it and make the wheels turn. There were no drag marks in the grass. What could explain this? Had the mower been teleported across the yard, or had it been picked up and carried? No one will probably ever know, but Randy estimated the weight of that mower at around 600 pounds. A quick Google search I did revealed it as being more like 800 to 900. Imagining that a bigfoot can deadlift that kind of weight and then carry it for sixty yards is truly staggering, but, then again, another Google search states that an African gorilla is twenty times stronger than a man and capable of lifting well over a thousand pounds. With that in mind, creatures nine and ten feet tall, such as the ones Randy has seen, must be almost unimaginably strong.

At the same time, Randy had just had a new garage built, and he found white finger marks strewn across the back of it. This had been a recurring thing, as he believed that something on the creature's skin left this white residue on anything it touched, and he'd seen it several times before. Were the creatures curious about the new building and felt the need to put their mark on it? Perhaps.

I made another visit to the place September 11 and 12, accompanied by a young friend of mine named Jake. He has interest in many paranormal subjects and was excited to experience the property, but he is also a rock musician, a member of three different bands in the Fargo area where we both live, so he related to Randy on that level, and the two of them easily hit it off talking about music and sound engineering and just every aspect of the business. Jake's musical style was spread across rock and roll, punk, and heavy metal, and I told him that Randy was in a boogie-woogie swing band. "Nothing wrong with that," he said. In a case of small world, it turned out the two had actually met before, when Randy was doing sound for a dance event in a northern Minnesota area, where Jake's girlfriend (now his wife) is from.

While giving us the standard tour of the property, since Jake was a first-time visitor, Randy showed us the poles along the powerline corridor where he'd previously found a lot of hair snagged, believed to be from the bigfoots using them to scratch their backs. Now there was something new on some of the poles—small V-shaped etchings in the wood that looked like they had been carved with a knife. This was impossible though, since Randy had not made them, and no one else ever came out there without his supervision. We speculated on whether the creatures would be able to do this with their fingernails. Jake and I then set up a tent to spend the night in at the nearby campfire area as Randy talked about all the findings and happenings out on the adjoining state land. He had an ATV known as a *side by side* that would only accommodate two people, so we decided he would take Jake out there for a look around while I stayed behind to rest for a bit in the tent. As I lay there in the late afternoon resting my eyes but still awake, I heard a sharp and unmistakable wood knock—just one—a short distance to the south. My eyes flew open, and I said to myself, "It begins." It wasn't even a surprise at this point, as so many sights and sounds had been experienced around this spot by so many people over the past few years. Shortly thereafter, I heard the ATV returning, and I greeted Randy and Jake. I told them what I'd heard, and they reported having found more V-shaped carvings in the state land. On what remained of that afternoon, Jake also said he heard the distant sound of a tree falling over.

We were hopeful for activity during the night as we sat around the campfire, but a sudden downpour put an end to things, and Jake and I ended up spending the night in the guest trailer near Randy's house instead of in the tent. The next morning, however, when we went out to take the tent down, we found a long red hair adhered to it, perhaps eighteen inches long. We had to think hard about this because, as Jake is a rock musician, he looks the part and has long hair, but his hair is brown, and the strand on the tent was distinctly red, matching the color of the nine-foot creature Randy had seen and named Big Red. It became just one more of the many hair samples collected on the property and seemed to suggest that Big Red might have come along during the night to check out our tent.

Big Red made another appearance, much more significant this time, later that same month, on September 27. Randy had a trail camera on a tree in the state land pointed toward the deer stand in which he and John Badger had had the sighting of the supposed dimensional portal and the creatures in orb form emerging from it. The camera was a considerable distance from the stand, which was beyond the range of its motion detector, so it had to be something closer to it that triggered it to take the picture that it did that day during daylight of a huge, reddish, upright figure that appeared to be on its knees at the base of the stand, with the back, head, and two arms clearly visible and raised up toward it with the elbows bent exactly where they should have been for this to be a picture of a real creature and not just an optical illusion of some kind. It has to be extremely zoomed in on to see the detail of the kneeling creature. In all honesty, it is what skeptics refer to as a "blobsquatch" photo, not nearly clear enough to prove anything, but those of us with a close connection to the case see it differently. I have wondered if the creature was reaching up to grab the stand in order to pull itself up from its crouch, or if it had its arms raised in some kind of demonstration of reverence for the site it was visiting. I also wonder if it was aware of the nearby camera and knew it was out of range of it, but that something like a bird flying by or something else that simple just happened to cause the camera to fire and capture the picture.

I would have loved to include that photo in this book, but it requires so much zooming in that I don't think it would translate very well in print.

On October 31, a sighting occurred that seemed to put to rest any doubt that there was something of a paranormal nature going on with the creatures around Randy's property. While on one of his daily walks around the place, he was hiking down the powerline corridor where he had had previous sightings, and, once again, he saw something a few poles distant from him—a huge, black, upright form standing next to the same pole where he'd previously seen both Big Red and the even bigger, black, ten-foot creature that others had also seen and seemed to be the same one he was seeing now. In his past sightings, he'd suffered from having to take his eyes off of what he was seeing just for brief moments and then having the creatures disappear from view, so this time, he was determined not to look away. As he advanced, he took out his phone and attempted to film what he was seeing. Perhaps he wasn't holding the phone high enough, but for whatever reason, it only captured images of the grass on the ground in front of him. Then, as he continued to stare at the giant creature, it suddenly just disappeared. There is no ambiguity about this. As he was looking right at it, he swears that it literally just vanished into thin air. No flash of light. No puff of smoke. Just, poof. It just blinked out. I have asked him if he thinks it just turned invisible and was actually still there, but he thinks it was literally gone.

As I was reacting to this report, Randy called to tell me about it. I said it was neat that he had had a sighting on Halloween, to which he seemed clueless and then said, "Oh yeah, it was Halloween, wasn't it?" His not realizing that the holiday was upon him seems to rule out any influence that the spooky season might have had on this sighting.

What can be said about a report like this? It is either made up, or it is evidence of something supernatural, and I have long since come to accept Randy as someone who is absolutely not a liar.

The rest of 2021 passed with occasional activity of a typical nature but no further sightings. A tangle of snapped branches behind Randy's house hinted at something clearing a line of sight to watch the property. The animal remains were eerily familiar—like the deer carcasses once scattered in the area, stripped of everything but hair—but now they were smaller: rabbits, and possibly even a bear.

A loud wood knock was heard, and black hair sixteen inches long was found snagged on a fence during deer hunting in November. In December, at a spot south of his place where he rarely visited, Randy found broken tree limbs lain across a trail, as if to block it with eighteen-inch footprints in the snow nearby, and also a small patch of blood, as if something had been killed. Incidents like this continued well into 2022; the activity showed no signs of slowing down.

The next thing to happen to me personally was in the summer of that year. On Friday, June 10, a few members of the SRA were having another visit, and I came up to join them, enthused about an idea I had for something to try. A reader of my book, *Sasquatch Central*, had suggested to me by email that I put a trail camera inside a closed container with some bait on top. That might entice a creature into opening the lid to see what might be inside, thereby triggering the camera to take a closeup shot of its face. Randy gave me permission to try it, and I brought a plastic tote, a jar of peanut butter, and a camera to carry it out. At first, I left all of this next to my tent, which was pitched at the far end of Randy's camping area from where his fire ring is. Then, in the early afternoon, after spending some time at the fire visiting with everyone, I went to set up my little experiment.

I took the tote with the camera inside it and the jar of peanut butter past the fire ring, toward the nearby river, and set them down for a moment so I could venture into a marshy area to check out a good spot to set them up. After deciding on a spot, I went and brought them into the marsh. In preparing to deploy, imagine my amazement when I opened the brand new peanut butter jar to peel the paper off the top only to find that the paper had been punched through. There was a big finger-scoop taken out of the peanut butter.

I went back to the fire and announced, "Guys, I just had something happen."

Everyone was excited and perplexed at something like this happening in broad daylight and so close to us as we all just sat here visiting. We traded reactions and ideas as we discussed it. I was thinking that it had happened in the few minutes between when I set the stuff down to venture into the marsh and when I returned. But, after a little more consideration, it seemed more likely that it had occurred during the couple of hours that all my gear was sitting outside my tent farther away, out of sight of the fire ring.

These bigfoots were long established as loving peanut butter and being able to remove and then replace the lids on jars, but having this happen to me personally was a somewhat emotional experience. It wasn't the first time I'd tried to fool them, or the first time they'd humbled me and put me in my place for it. I still set the little camera trap out in the marsh for the rest of the day with the jar on top of the tote, but nothing resulted from it.

"A swing and a miss," quipped SRA head Todd Newby, who was there, and we shared a laugh over it.

There was one more clue to be found, though, when we examined my campsite where the peanut butter had most likely been tampered with. I had a cooler next to my tent, and on the ground a few yards from it was the aluminum lid from a can of Spam, which I'd taken out and put back in the cooler earlier to make a sandwich. The lid was somewhat more curled than the shape I'd left it in, and it had evidently been taken out by whatever had messed with the peanut butter, curiously not touching the Spam itself but just the lid and then reclosing the cooler. I collected the lid and have kept it in

cold storage ever since, just in case it
was licked and there might be DNA
on it.

I slept in my tent that night,
anxious that something more might
happen, but nothing did.

Something did happen the next
night, however, when I decided to
sleep in my car, which was parked
about fifty feet from Randy's house.
Brian Glynn had come out that night
to join the search, opting to sit in his
preferred deer stand, not far from the
campfire area and river, where he would often sit for hours and just
watch and listen. Everyone but him was retired for the night by
shortly after midnight, but as I lay sleeping fitfully in my car at about
4:30 AM, I suddenly found myself groggily awoken and hearing
mysterious sounds coming from the direction of the house. I heard a
combination of growls and a gruff throat-clearing type of sound,
rising and falling in pitch, unlike anything I'd ever heard. As near as I
could tell, it was coming from about the spot on the side of the house
that the creatures occasionally pounded on. It suddenly dawned on
me that there was likely a bigfoot standing fifty feet away from me
and that it didn't know I was inside the car, so I decided not to sit up
and expose myself but just listened for a moment until the sounds
stopped, and I eventually faded back to sleep.

In the morning, I learned that I was not the only one to hear
those sounds. After hours of observation, Brian Glynn had come
down from the tree stand at nearly 4:30 to leave for the night, and at
that same time, Randy's wife, Teri, was preparing to leave for work,
where she had an early morning shift at a nursing home in Blackduck. They were both outside the house at around the same time,
and they both heard the same sounds I did. Brian believed that a
bigfoot had followed him from the deer stand back to the house. It
had turned out to be a dramatic weekend for me. I'd experienced

things on a personal level, including my possessions being interfered with and what was by far the closest vocalization I had ever heard.

But there is no more emotional Bigfoot encounter than an actual sighting, and the next one happened just a week later, when Teri finally had a frightening look at one of the creatures. She was never a doubter of what her husband and other people had been reporting all around the place but had chosen to stay out of it, content to let whoever come and investigate but opting to never venture out into the woods herself and hoping to never be confronted by what haunted the property. That changed for her on the night of June 18, when she was driving home from work. As she approached the driveway, she saw illuminated in her headlights a huge, dark, hairy creature—surmised to be the big ten-footer—crouched down at the side of the highway. Surprisingly, it did not stand up and run off as she neared it. Instead, it just stayed put, watching as her car rolled past at a distance of only a few feet, affording her an excellent view that she had never wanted to have. She did not stop but turned into the driveway and then continued on to the house, where she hurried inside in fear. When she told Randy what she'd seen, she referred to a small Bigfoot statue Randy had bought and decoration their living room with. "It looked just like the statue," she said. Teri joined her daughter, Samantha, that night in being witness to one of the creatures along the road at the edge of the property.

The final weekend of July afforded me another opportunity to experience some major activity. On Saturday 30, I went up to join Randy and two young Native American men from a nearby reservation. They had heard about his story and asked to come and check it out. As I recall, one of them had read my book. It was a particularly hot summer day, over ninety degrees, and as we were going to be hiking out to explore the state land, we knew to bring a lot of water.

When we got to the large teepee structure out there, we stopped to both take in its awesomeness and also to take a rest break, sitting down and drinking water before moving on. One of the Native men had occasionally been taking random pictures with his phone, over his shoulder and in other directions, just in case something signifi-

The statue said to look almost exactly like the creature Teri saw.

cant might show up in one of them. We continued on, and nothing of note happened, but when those pictures were scrolled through later, there was one from that rest break by the teepee that did stand out. It showed a black figure through green brush, mostly obscured but with certain features apparent; in particular, a face that can only be described as a cross between apelike and humanlike. Deep-set dark eyes and a wide nose are clearly visible, while the mouth is covered by overhanging leaves. Above the eyes is a heavy brow ridge. Above that, the head seems to terminate where one would expect to see a much higher skull. It's a perplexing image, but whatever it was, it was standing just a few yards away from us during our rest break, though none of us saw or heard a thing.

The Native men left at the end of that day, but I stayed for one more night, during which, Randy and I heard distant vocalizations while sitting around the campfire. But, whereas before such sounds had always been like deep male voices, these now sounded like females or children. It is hard to describe these because they were fleeting—just snippets of sound. I slept in my car again that night in front of the

Possible creature photo from July 30, 2022. Is this a picture of Bigfoot?

house, but after Randy had gone to bed, I was lingering in the late night, leaning against the front of my car just listening to the night, and there was one moment where I heard one more quick burst of sound, just a few seconds of gibberish that seemed to be coming from the area of the campfire ring and which had a distinctly female sound to it. I find this fascinating, as there is no animal I know of besides humans whose male and female voices share the same distinctions.

A few weeks later, in August, Randy was once again watching over Samantha's daughters, Bristol and Madison. They were out at his peanut butter gifting area when they heard growling that was not like a bear's and then movement in the nearby brush. With the girls' safety in mind, Randy immediately led them away, and when they talked about it, Randy said he had only heard breaking brush, but the kids said they had heard actual footsteps.

When summer turned to autumn, on the night of October 24, Samantha got off work in Blackduck at 11:00 and stopped by on her way home to visit with her mother. As the two were talking out in the yard at about 11:30, they heard three loud whoops from the direction of the river. Teri headed back into the house, but Samantha got back in her car and left posthaste.

The next day, Randy found a fawn that had been killed by a car near his driveway on the highway and moved its body into the woods. Late that night, he and Teri were awakened by loud howling very close to the house, obviously not the familiar sound of the coyotes that lived in the area that were heard all the time, but more long and drawn out and with barking-type sounds that would merge into a howl. It was similar to a recording captured back in October 2020 during a visit by Minnesota Bigfooter Abe DelRio and his brother, Nick, when an early morning howl had coincided with eighteen-inch footprints leading away across the powerline corridor in frost that soon melted away from the rising sun. The next day, Randy went to check the body of the fawn and found that its heart and liver had been neatly removed, but it was otherwise intact—completely unnatural for any kind of normal predator or scavenger, but identical to a couple of other deer he had found in the past. Usually, what he found with deer kills was just masses of hair left on the ground, but, occasionally, the creatures evidently chose to do this bizarre act of leaving the bodies intact except for removing two specific internal organs.

On December 11, Randy and friend, John Badger, were exploring the state land, and Randy spoke out loud that he'd like to hear some tree knocks, not shouting, but merely in a conversational voice. A moment later, both men heard six loud knocks, the loudest they'd ever heard, from sixty or seventy yards away. Randy was realizing more and more that the creatures were responding directly to things he would say to them, and noting that something as huge as they were could not be simply hiding nearby behind some poplar tree without being seen. He was coming to understand that they were not hearing him conventionally, but from some other plane of existence; not only that, but also perfectly understanding his words. He was far past thinking that they were simple flesh and blood animals, but things like this cemented that belief even further for him.

We now move into the year 2023. On January 16, Randy was exploring deep into the woods when he found a typical deer-kill site —small in size, indicating a fawn had been killed—with nothing but hair remaining, something he'd seen many times. But this time, there was a Bigfoot track in the snow at the edge of the hair. Just one, with no more evident anywhere in the vicinity. It begs the question, how does anything leave just one footprint in snow? Where did it come from? Where did it go? There were also no apparent signs of a struggle. The paranormal aspect of the case teases the imagination into picturing a bigfoot's method of targeting deer being just to suddenly materialize next to them and take them out in an instant rather than spending time stalking them. Every time I say something like that, I have to dwell on how crazy it sounds, but the evidence is what it is. Randy also found and photographed another deer kill in the area at that time that he believed was done by a natural predator of some kind—a wolf or cougar—that showed a bloody spine and other eviscerated remains in order to show the difference.

Further evidence featuring the mystery of how something so huge could avoid leaving tracks in snow occurred on February 5 when Randy found strands of red hair snagged on a powerline pole. This was a common occurrence in the summer, when he believed the creatures liked to scratch their backs on the poles to rid themselves of bugs, but it had never happened in winter before. Strangely, there were no tracks in the snow around the poles. Clearly, even if the hair had come from some other animal, there should have been tracks.

Two days later, Randy had a major track find in the area of the river and the deer stand that Brian Glynn favored as a stakeout spot whenever he would visit, a hundred yards or so from the campfire ring. He had no measuring device with him, but the prints were about fifty percent longer than his glove and had a huge stride. There were many of them for a change, leading toward the barbed wire fence of the neighbor's pasture that adjoined his land and then crossing it without breaking stride. Also, white hair six or seven inches long was found snagged on the top wire. This is intriguing, as no white creatures had been seen on the property. But then, just as before, after crossing the fence, the tracks just ended in an open area.

At around this same time, Randy took one of his dogs out into his back yard, and they heard a loud exhalation of breath come from nearby in the woods that frightened the dog into wanting to flee back into the house.

March passed uneventfully, but on April 1, while Randy was exploring by snowmobile, he found another deer kill with a typical large mass of hair but also two severed deer legs, one of them pulled out of the hip joint, with no teeth marks on them. Most strangely, once again, although there were many deer tracks in the snow surrounding the site, there were no tracks of whatever had made the kill.

Five days later, as Randy was on one of his usual walks in the woods and speaking out loud to the creatures, assuming they could hear and understand him, he asked them to pound on his house, which was something they'd done several times but not in a while. That night, it did indeed happen, not just once but twice, the first time being in the spot they usually pounded on but the second being on the opposite side of the house. It caused the dogs to growl fiercely.

And as it was becoming no surprise now, no tracks were found in the snow around the house.

On April 13, Randy, while exploring, found an incredible nine deer-kill sites, an unprecedented number, as that had once been about how many he would find in a whole year. A few seemed to be the work of wolves or coyotes, but most were of the type he believed to be done by Bigfoot, with nothing left but hair. And again, at those sites, there were no tracks in the snow.

On April 21, Randy found wolf signs near his house in the snow and, while following it, he briefly caught site of the wolf, then found a dead deer that it had been sniffing around but not feeding on. This was very close to the site where, in an SRA visit to the property in September of 2020, team member Andy Peiper and two others had seen an enormous, black, upright figure cross a trail just a few yards in front of them in the dark of night. This kill was of the rare kind, not typical of normal predators, as it wasn't torn apart and so seeming to be indicative of a bigfoot but being intact with just slight damage done to it, which only happened once in a great while. One leg was broken, and the ribs were torn open with the heart and liver extracted, but the neck was also broken this time. This tenth deer kill in April showed drag marks in the snow where the body had been moved fifteen feet, but—again, no surprise—there were no tracks and not even any blood to be seen. This kill happened a frighteningly close distance from Randy's house.

What can one make of this business of such dramatic activity going on in snowy conditions where nothing should be able to avoid leaving tracks but where there just aren't any? There is much speculation about the creatures being of a paranormal nature, but it usually involves a belief that they are physical and flesh and blood while they are on the Earth plane but are able to merge in and out between it and some other dimension. They leave tracks and hair behind, they feed on deer, they make tree structures and damage property—all physical attributes that seem to suggest that even if they are paranormal, they have to obey the laws of our physical world while they are in it. So, their habit of so often not leaving tracks in snow while they are performing physical acts while on our side of the matrix just seems to make no sense at all. I do not pretend to have any idea what I am talking about as I speculate about this.

A frightening incident occurred on the night of April 24. While Randy and Teri were asleep in their bedroom, Teri was awakened at about 11 PM by five screams outside. The motion sensor light outside the bedroom window had also come on, even though the screams seemed to be coming from the area where the deer kill lay from three days earlier. These sounds woke her, even though a fan was running in the room for noise insulation. She woke Randy, and for the next thirty to forty-five minutes, they listened to a whole series of intense vocalizations that repeated every minute and a half or so—grunts, growls, screams, barks, a cacophony of sounds. Near the end, there were just grunts like those of an ape, and then it finally stopped.

More activity happened in May. The house was again pounded on at night, and then bizarre poltergeist-type things started to happen, as had occasionally taken place over the years since the entire Bigfoot episode had begun but not been a constant thing. A radio in the house started to come on by itself, even after being unplugged. The sound bar on Randy's TV became all messed up and had to be reprogrammed. The settings on the position of the driver's seat in his pickup truck were somehow changed and had to be readjusted. Randy thought back to how he had invited the creatures to visit the house back in April, so now he went out to the woods and spoke to them again and said that their visits were scaring his wife, so could they please stop. And immediately, the things in the house did indeed stop.

The supernatural-type things that happen on the property in addition to the Bigfoot activity are rife for speculation. It seems impossible that huge hairy creatures could actually be entering the house, and psychics who have evaluated the case have concluded that, in addition to the bigfoots, there are nature spirits in the land that have become hyperactive because of the creatures' presence and actually are the ones responsible for some of the weirder aspects of what is going on. Trying to convince skeptics that Bigfoot exists seems to become ten times harder when such supernatural elements are added into the mix, but the story is what it is.

In May, Randy had just sold a large camper he owned and bought a new smaller one, the kind designed to be towed behind a pickup truck. It was a handy thing to have, both for himself to stay in when he would travel to musical gigs, or for guests staying nights at his place. New things coming on to the property often seemed to attract the attention of the creatures, and once it was there, Randy started finding the camper's door locked when he knew he had left it unlocked, which could not happen accidentally but required the doorknob to be pushed in and turned.

One day, Randy was cleaning the new trailer, just inside the open door down on his hands and knees, using a vacuum cleaner, when in his peripheral, he saw something large and black pass by the doorway outside just inches away. At first, he thought it was Teri, who happened to be wearing black at the time, but when he looked up and out, she was not there, and neither was anyone else. He believed a black Bigfoot had just walked by, boldly approaching that close to him in broad daylight, and if so, that would make it his seventh sighting. He and I actually have kind of an amusing disagreement about that number because, since he once had a sighting of two creatures in the form of orbs coming out of a portal, he considers that to be two sightings at once, making his total number eight. The way I see it though, that was a single sighting of two beings, not two simultaneous sightings.

Just after the trailer sighting, I made another visit on the weekend of May 12 and 13 and ended up having some very profound experiences. In June of 2022, I'd had the occurrence of a creature apparently going into a cooler at my campsite and messing with foodstuffs, and this time, it actually happened again. My tent and other gear were set up at the same spot as before, a hundred yards or so from the campfire area and not visible from it, and, as Randy, Tanner and I sat by the fire in the early afternoon I decided to go over and get my cooler and bring it back to make some sandwiches. As we were all just casually talking, I took out a plastic jar of mayonnaise and then immediately said, "Um, I don't remember there being a dent in this jar like this." All eyes then focused on the jar, which looked like something had squeezed it. When I then took out a package of baloney that had also had this done to it, with multiple clear finger impressions on one side of it and a single thumbprint on the other, pandemonium struck. What could it mean, besides a creature once again invading my campsite and cooler, investigating the contents, and then closing it again? Nothing was eaten, and bread and cheese in the cooler were apparently untouched.

Excited, the three of us went over to my campsite to look around. As we approached it, a wood knock—or at least what is commonly thought to be a wood knock—came from the nearby woods, loud and sharp and easily within fifty yards of us, but unlike any that any of us had heard before. It was multiple impacts within a few seconds, rapid fire like a machine gun burst. I can just hear the skeptics insisting that it must have been a woodpecker, but it was most definitely not. I am familiar with the sounds of those birds, and they are nowhere near as loud as this was. When we reached the campsite, Randy thought he could make out a possible foot-shaped impression in the grass right where my cooler had been sitting, but we couldn't be certain.

That night after visiting around the fire for a while, Randy and Tanner went back to the house at around 9:30, and I remained to watch and listen by myself. On and off, we'd been hearing the sounds of cows in the far distance in their pasture on Randy's neighbor's property. Sometimes, the cows were in pasture land immediately adjacent to Randy's land, where I had heard them before being disturbed by what I believed to have been a bigfoot, but for now, they were being contained about half a mile away. About an hour after Randy and Tanner left, something happened that absolutely mystifies me, because I can't believe how calmly I reacted to it. Something slowly approached me at the fire from out of the woods, growling. It was an unmistakable sound, deep and guttural, much like that of a bear, and for all I knew, that might well have been what it was at first, but then, twice during the approximately four minutes that it went on, it did something most unbearlike. The growling suddenly rose in pitch and then morphed into a thundering bellow that sounded exactly like one of the cows I knew to be a half mile away, but this was less than fifty yards from me, yet just out of sight in the darkness.

Foodstuffs squeezed and dented from inside my cooler.

After those few minutes, it just ended, with no sound of footsteps or any other sign of the thing's departure. Randy had told me to talk to the bigfoots the way he always did, so, in the same manner as him, I called out, "Hey, you guys, was that you? That was really cool." The rest of the night was quiet and uneventful.

I still can't believe that during this incident, I just sat there by the fire calmly listening. The memory has a surreal feeling to it, as if whatever was doing it had somehow put me into a lethargic state. I simply didn't feel that I was in any danger. Skeptics might suggest that a neighbor's cow had escaped and had come close to do the bellowing, but it goes without saying that cows do not growl. I don't know what to make of this incident. I believe it to have been a bigfoot making those sounds, and I'd like to think that it meant that they were starting to be willing to approach me, but it could have just as easily been a threat. It was a unique experience, to be sure.

The next day, there was a visit by two members of Itasca County Bigfoot Research, Zac Malmquist and Jeremy Olson. They were both young, strapping, and rugged outdoorsmen who had been in touch with Randy and were eager to check his place out. The two of them accompanied Randy and me on a long hike out to the state land, where, quite unexpectedly, we found the seventeenth and eighteenth deer kills of that year so far. It was the same as most times, just a carpeting on the ground of deer hair without any other remains.

Zac and Jeremy had some impressive technology at their disposal and sent up a flying drone to survey the whole area around Randy's property. It was exciting to see the aerial footage the drone captured for miles around, but it didn't pick up any evidence of Bigfoot. That was no surprise, since the thick forest canopy prevented a clear look at the ground from above.

I think the Itasca County boys left that day with the impression that Randy's place was a great but challenging Bigfoot hotspot.

A couple of weeks later, it was time for the all-female She-Squatchers team to become involved with Randy's story. I had introduced Randy and the Shes' leader, Jen Kruse, at the previous annual Minnesota Bigfoot Conference in Grand Rapids, and they had been going back and forth about getting this visit together. In March, they had had Randy as a guest on their weekly *Journey Radio Show* podcast, in which they'd expressed great interest in his story and the intention to come and check things out for themselves. Subsequently, Randy would appear twice more on the show by popular demand. In retrospect, now I'm quite proud of myself for making that introduction, because the things that have resulted from it are absolute gold.

Randy and Zac Malmquist examine evidence during the Itasca County Researchers' visit, including a deer-kill site with only hair remaining.

On the weekend of May 31 to June 1, Jen Kruse and her best friend and sidekick, Jena Grover, came to Randy's place to spend time exploring and assessing it for a documentary film they had plans to be taking part in in the near future. The third member of their team, Tammy Treichel, was not able to take part because, though originally from the area, she was now living on the East Coast in Virginia, but she planned to join her teammates in the production once filming of the documentary started. I was there with everyone, happy and excited to be included in this exploratory adventure.

I arrived first at Randy's, and we waited for the Shes to get there. I had passed through some annoying road construction on the way up, and they messaged me that they were now dealing with it too. Once they finally arrived, we gathered for a gracious meeting in the camper in Randy's yard, in which the girls were planning to be staying. The fun-loving natures and senses of humor of Randy and the girls immediately clicked, and it was a joy to be part of. After some initial conversation, Randy led us out on a tour of his property that began where the powerline corridor cut through. There, he had a couple of flatbed trailers where he was displaying all the animal skulls and Y-sticks that he had found and believed had been gifted to him by Bigfoot. From there, we continued on up the corridor, where he led us into the nearby woods to point out some small stick structures, and then back out to the powerline to reveal the poles that regularly had what was believed to be Bigfoot hair snagged on them from the creatures scratching their backs. I had seen all of this many times before, but it was a thrill to watch the Shes taking it in for the first time. Then, however, something most unexpected happened.

As Jena was kneeling, intensely studying the pole, we were standing by and taking video of the hairs stuck to it, and Randy was continuing to narrate his story. Jen was staring farther up the corridor, and she suddenly cut in. She said that when we had first entered the corridor, she had seen something dark and vertical next to a pole far up the powerline that had immediately struck her as looking like it might be a bigfoot, but that since neither Randy or I had said anything or seemed to notice it that she'd assumed it must be just a dead tree or some other natural object. Now, however, when she looked down at the same spot, the figure was gone. Upon hearing this, Jena snapped out of her intense focus on the hair samples and basically said, "Wait a minute—what? I saw something too." And as we talked, it turned out they'd each seen a dark figure standing beside the powerline, but not the same one. The one Jen had seen was to the left of the line and about ten-feet tall, based on its position next to a black plastic wrap that all the poles have at a ten-foot level to prevent animals from climbing the poles, while the one Jena saw was a couple of feet shorter and to the right of the line. Both women had assumed they were looking at dead trees, since Randy and I didn't seem to notice, but now both figures had apparently walked away. It was a frantic moment as we realized that two Bigfoot sightings had just happened simultaneously in the same spot and that Randy and I had missed out just because we didn't happen to be looking at the exact spot at the time. Also significant, the pole both supposed Bigfoots were standing near was the same one Randy had seen them by three times before. It seemed incredible that Jen and Jena could both have creature sightings less than an hour after arriving at the property, but the She-Squatchers are a team of psychics with the gift of more than just five senses.

Randy continued to give the usual tour of his property, showing the Shes multiple stick structures and his gifting area, where he regularly left peanut butter jars whose lids had been left on the ground, arranged according to color by whatever was eating the peanut butter. It was there that Jen decided to leave a gift from her heritage for the creatures, a bit of traditional Ojibwa tobacco that she named as *kinnikinnick*. Within a couple of days, Randy would announce that this tobacco gift was gone. But for now, we then came to the campfire area beside the river, where we planned to be spending much of the night and where much Bigfoot activity had taken place. The next step was to venture out to the state land. Jena was gung ho for that hike, but Jen didn't feel up to it, so Randy guided Jena out to the deep woods while I stayed behind to keep Jen company. Both ladies are fun-loving, but Jen is a bit more serious, while Jena is bubbly and, I dare say, kind of the comic relief of the group (I say that with the utmost respect, because she is delightful).

It was late afternoon when Randy and Jena returned after viewing the large teepee structure and other things in the state land. Randy praised Jena's energy, telling me, "Boy, she really held her own out there." After getting something to eat, we started back toward the campfire area in the evening, but by this time, ominous storm clouds had begun to creep in that gave us great concern. Trying to be optimistic, Randy said it looked like it would bypass us as we continued on, but that went out the window as we reached the campfire area as the sky opened up in a torrential downpour. We ran for the large deer stand that rests there and sheltered underneath it, pulling out camp chairs stored there and making the best of our suddenly soaked situation and spending a couple of hours there as we waited for the storm to pass. It was the kind of thing one laughs about later.

Randy and the She-Squatchers explore the powerline corridor and the nearby woods.

The storm did pass, and in its aftermath, we got a campfire going and spent a few hours sitting around it in the hopes of having some Bigfoot activity. Sure enough, there came a point late at night when, in addition to coyotes howling, we heard distant sounds re like human voices coming from the direction of the powerline. It was an experience I'd had there before, and now I got to share it with Randy and the Shes, looking at them and going, "You hear that, right?" and having them answer yes.

Following that, we decided to go on a little flashlight hike across the bridges that spanned the nearby river, as Randy pointed out a couple of spots along the fence line there where various things had happened. As we looked around in the dark, Jen asked Randy if there were reflectors attached to some fenceposts fifty yards or so down the line. He said no, but as we all looked, there were now small points of light showing in our flashlight beams that began to move and bob about. There was so much movement, in fact, that there was no doubt we were looking at something alive. It was an exciting moment, as we wondered if we might be looking at a small number of Bigfoot creatures, but, eventually, Randy said he could make out the hindquarters of a deer walking away, and so the mystery was solved. After that, we called it a night and headed back to where we were staying around the house, with the girls in the camper and myself in the guest trailer.

Before parting company the next day, we all went into Black-duck to share a big meal together at a café, a gathering that included Randy's stepson, Tanner, and his granddaughters, Bristol and Madison, who had both had Bigfoot sightings. It was charming seeing the She-Squatchers interacting with the kids and asking about their experiences, but things had changed a bit. Bristol had been nine years old when she and Randy had seen a creature together in 2020. She'd been willing to talk about it then, but now, at twelve, she was a tween and becoming more aloof and seeming to prefer leaving it behind her. Meanwhile, Randy was relating a story about how little Madison had been out in the woods with him while he was looking for evidence, and how she'd said out loud, "Sasquatch, we mean you no harm. We love you. We just want to see you." He wished he'd been recording, and the Shes found it charming. But Madison reacted by closing her eyes, covering her ears, and shaking her head insistently back and forth. "No, I didn't say that." Bless her little heart; she was embarrassed. It was a funny and heartwarming way to end our visit that weekend as we all went our ways.

Despite her once having tried to express friendliness to the creatures, little Madison would have another frightening experience just a few weeks later, on June 21. She was in the front yard near the deck of the house at about 2 PM and saw the black ten-foot creature standing at the edge of the woods near the guest trailer. That is a distance, but not a comfortable or safe one for a young child to see something like that. It was in sight for just a few seconds and then disappeared, with uncertainness over whether it just stepped into the trees or vanished into thin air, as Randy had previously witnessed. No one could be sure when Madison ran into the house and told what she'd seen, but this was her third sighting. I can't help but have my heart go out to such a young child being subjected to such things while visiting her family. I sincerely hope she isn't teased about it in school or doesn't suffer any emotional trauma as she gets older.

Just a week later, on June 28, Randy set up the camper in his yard for Bristol and Madison to stay in and decided to move it closer to the garage and farther from the house. Shortly after, while Randy was away from home, Teri, Tanner, and the girls all heard a noise outside so loud that they heard it over the fans running in the house. It was the sound of the camper door being struck by an open hand, which made a big dent with impressions of fingertips. The creatures had already seemed to express an interest in the camper, and now they appeared upset about it being moved.

Over the next few days, as he pondered what was going on with the trailer, Randy took a couple of opportunities to sit in deer stands at night and watch and listen, as he often did. On the night of July 2, as he sat in the one near where he and John Badger had had their experience with the portal and the orbs, he heard loud wood knocks in the nearby woods. There were six knocks twice, three knocks once, what sounded like bipedal walking, and a deer doing a lot of agitated snorting. Randy could tell the deer was not smelling him, because he was downwind from it.

Four nights later, he was in a different tree stand after putting out some apples for bait. He heard just one tree knock, and then something downright weird happened. There was a particular apple within sight in the dark, and it seemed to just vanish while he was looking at it. There is ambiguity as to whether he took his eyes off it for a few seconds or not, but even if he did, that was one fast disappearance.

These seemed to be minor but tantalizing events to keep the story going, until July 16, when the camper in the yard again became the focus of attention. Bristol, Madison, and their mother, Samantha, had had some private events in their life that caused a shakeup in their living conditions, and they needed a place to stay for a while, so they were all sleeping in the camper at night when something presumed to be a bigfoot suddenly shook it so roughly that it fell off the concrete block holding it level, jolting everyone awake and causing quite a scare. Nothing else happened that night, but it makes me feel for their little family, whose every member had already had such fearful Bigfoot experiences. Not going into the woods anymore had become a rule, but not even the front yard seemed safe now. How scary it must have been to realize that one or more creatures had been only a few feet from them. I've had that experience myself, so I can relate.

It's purely speculation on my part, of course, but it seems that the creatures were intent on maintaining a kind of status quo here and were basically saying, you are not usually here, and we don't like that you're here now. Change is bad.

If that was the case, it seems odd that the creatures seemed to keep their involvement to a minimum—not staying hidden, but nothing overtly scary—when a big shakeup happened from Thursday August 10 to Sunday 13. Over that weekend, the She-Squatchers returned to Randy's property for the documentary film shoot they had done reconnaissance for during their previous visit in May, when only Jen Kruse and Jena Grover had been present, but now their third member, Tammy Treichel, who lived far away in Virginia, was also in attendance, as well as the film's producer, Jason Kenzie. Jason was a noted filmmaker and photojournalist from British Columbia, Canada, who had a long history of making wildlife documentaries and had more recently turned his interest toward cryptozoology, especially Bigfoot. Footage he would shoot in this Minnesota region with the Shes would become the latest installments in his ongoing documentary series, *Searching for Sasquatch*. Jason always wore a khaki shirt and kind of reminded me of Steve Irwin, the Crocodile Hunter, but never getting into as much danger as Irwin had. Rounding out the team was Jason's cameraman and paranormal investigator, Todd Schelat. And then, of course, there was me. I wasn't sure what role, if any, I would play beyond observing, but it reminded me of the previous visits by the SRA, in which such a mixed bag of creature activity had occurred, so I was excited to take part.

Observing the filmmaking process over those few days was very interesting. Jason took a lighthearted and somewhat skeptical approach to the subject and tried to inject humor into it, which put me off a bit. At the same time, he was respectful of everyone, and it was clear he was a professional who knew what he was doing. Some dramatic overhead footage was filmed via drone under controlled conditions, and some sequences that seemed like spontaneous activity were actually staged and sometimes took a couple of takes to get them just right. I was part of this. As it turned out, I did get to appear in the film, both out doing field work and in a sit-down interview. Controlled conditions were mixed with field filming, in which anything might happen, and happen it did, including a moment in which Randy, Jason, Todd, and myself were out in the state land near the big teepee structure and accidentally disturbed a nest full of wasps that started swarming and sent us running away. Luckily, we avoided being stung.

I didn't arrive on site until the second day, and one of the first spontaneous things to happen was on the first, when Tammy, along with the rest of the She-Squatchers, was having her first walk up the powerline corridor. Just as Jen and Jena had experienced three months before, Tammy looked down toward the power pole, beside which multiple sightings now had been made before and at considerable distance caught a brief glimpse of what looked like a huge dark creature sticking its head and upper body out of the nearby tree line. She estimated it was ten or even twelve feet in height, but an examination of the spot later revealed it might have been hanging from trees a couple of feet above ground. That all three She-Squatchers had now had sightings almost immediately upon arriving on the property seemed almost beyond belief, but I am in no position to question it, as I firmly support these women's veracity. There is an energy at this place that almost seems to single out individuals who are meant to see things. Perhaps it is the same energy that occasionally interferes with electronics, causing fully charged batteries to instantly drain in phones and cameras. That would also happen to Tammy during this weekend, as there was a moment when she felt dizzy and heavy, as if the pull of gravity had suddenly increased, then found that her wristwatch, whose battery had been fully charged, had abruptly gone dead.

Tammy's first glimpse wasn't the only sighting that weekend. On my first day there, the girls and I were pitching our tents just yards from each other in a spot close to Randy's campfire area, and there came a moment where just myself, Tammy, and cameraman Todd were there, when I found a hole in my air mattress. Todd offered to go off to where he was camping to get some duct tape. While I was alone with Tammy waiting for him to get back, something very odd happened. We were at a juncture of two trails, and Tammy glimpsed something through the brush coming down a trail, movement of some kind of a figure that looked about to emerge on our trail, but then it didn't. She even called out, "Oh, here comes somebody," and assumed it was either Todd or one of the other She-Squatchers, but no one appeared. No explanation was found for what she had seen.

Jason Kenzie examines a stick structure near Randy's peanut butter
gifting area.

Later that same day, we were all in that same general area on the trails on a spot close to the river, and I was standing next to Jen when I noticed her suddenly staring intently into the woods with a quizzical look. When I turned to look where she was looking, I saw a tree branch bouncing up and down, which had clearly just been bumped by something passing by it. Jen said she had caught a second's glimpse of something large and black moving past that tree. I have to say, it was kind of a mental struggle to come to grips with the fact that the She-Squatchers had now had five sightings at this place, four of which I had been present for without seeing what they saw in spite of standing right there. I try not to view it as frustrating though, but rather as exciting and as motivation to continue to visit the property.

After dark, I accompanied Jason and the girls in flashlight hiking in the woods, and we came across a vaguely lean-to-type structure of small sticks a few feet long that were stacked up neatly side by side. Jena closely examined them and determined that none of them were rooted there and wondered if they could have fallen there naturally. Even skeptical Jason said no; there was no way they could have fallen that neatly and close together. Shortly beyond there, we found an impressive and large spiderweb-like tree structure that Randy had not yet seen himself. There was also a funny moment, when we saw eyeshine ten feet up and got briefly excited, until we realized it was just a raccoon in a tree.

When it came time to bed down for the night, the Shes and I were in our tents, and the night passed uneventfully, but as the sun was rising in the early morning, there was a sudden outburst of noise. To me, it sounded like bellowing cows with a dog barking at them, but once we all woke and emerged from our tents, the girls asked me if I'd heard "those howls" and said they'd recorded them. I said that what I'd heard sounded more like cows and a dog, but as I woke up further and thought about it, I remembered that the nearest cows were fairly far away and shouldn't sound as close as they did. I wondered if what we'd heard were the same kind of mimicked sounds I'd heard before in this same spot.

When the filming came to an end, we all said our goodbyes after having shared an amazing adventure. Jason, Todd, and the She-Squatchers continued on farther north to the Red Lake Indian Reservation, where Jen is a registered band member, to do more exploration into the widespread Bigfoot activity there before their time together came to an end. Two episodes of Jason's *Searching for Sasquatch* series came out of that weekend, both containing footage from Randy's place. I was featured in the one titled *The Minnesota Roars*. This had to do with a recording of supposed Bigfoot vocalizations that had been made available to the She-Squatchers.

The recording was said to have been made by an elderly man leaving a recorder on his back porch "near Itasca." I wondered at first what exactly that meant, because in northern Minnesota there is both Itasca State Park, which features the headwaters of the Mississippi River, and Itasca County. The park is not located in that county, which sometimes confuses people. However, I have confirmed with Jen Kruse that the location is in northern Hubbard County on private property not far from the Mississippi headwaters. The narrative stated that the location was only "a few miles" from Randy's property, but that was a bit of dramatic license, as Itasca State Park is around sixty miles from Blackduck.

The Minnesota Roars recording is amazing, equal, in my opinion, to any of the best Bigfoot audios I've heard. There is a loud, powerful, low-pitched, guttural roar at first that must be very close to the recorder. It's then joined by farther creatures uttering higher-pitched screams and howls for several minutes. In a scene in the documentary, in which the sounds are being listened to around a picnic table in Randy's yard, Jason speculates that it sounds like at least a half dozen creatures and that the loudest one closest to the recorder definitely sounds "angry." The fact that Tammy then immediately chimes in with "Or hurt" seems poignant to me, a recognition that first emotional impressions might not necessarily be accurate. Randy commented that it was one of the best recordings he'd ever heard and that, while he'd captured several of his own, they were all from a much greater distance.

Getting to take part in this documentary and even having my name featured in the credits was, of course, a fun adventure, but when it was over, the activity at Randy's continued. Usually, it was minor things like sounds or the little items he would regularly leave out by his campfire area being moved around in a constant little game he believed he and the creatures were playing with each other. But on Wednesday, October 11, he would have his closest and possibly most dramatic sighting ever. I suppose that's a matter of opinion, but I know that when he first told me of it, I was blown away.

He was out at his peanut butter gifting area, not too far from his house, as late afternoon was turning to evening. As he always did, he spoke out loud to the creatures and told them he was going to go and sit in a nearby tree stand for a while. As he did so, and as dusk approached, he was suddenly struck by an intense dizzy spell, his vision out of focus, and it made him double over and close his eyes in confusion. While in this position, he heard a couple of footsteps in the dry leaves carpeting the forest floor right next to the stand. He opened his eyes and stood up straight to see what it was. This tree stand had him surrounded by a wooden structure that didn't allow him to see down to the ground, but just above it and just inches away, a huge Bigfoot head was passing by. This happened in just seconds, but Randy said it was so close that he could have reached out and touched it. The head was in profile, with reddish brown hair and a face that looked like a wrinkled old man, and the one eye he could see was big and black. Despite the entire forest floor being covered in dry leaves, he only heard a couple of footsteps, and then it was over, and the creature was gone. The fact that Randy is matter-of-fact about this and not overwhelmed with emotion over such an experience is impressive. I don't think I would be able to do the same if such a thing was to happen to me. This happened to be the twenty-eighth creature sighting on the property by not just Randy but so many other witnesses, an impressive grand total that showed no signs of ending any time soon. It made me wonder if he had built up such a level of trust with the creatures that they were now willing to come that intensely close to him.

Incidentally, the size of this creature compared to the height of the tree stand made Randy estimate its height at about ten and a half feet, and he couldn't be sure if it was one of the ones he'd sighted previously or not.

Several weeks later, on December 11, Randy called me to report that he'd had a few more episodes of blurry vision and dizziness while out in the woods, and it had concerned him enough to go and get checked out by an eye doctor, but the diagnosis was that his eyes were perfectly healthy.

Things were relatively quiet for a couple of months, until an incident occurred on New Year's Day of 2024. Randy's stepson ,Tanner, took the dogs out of the house to relieve themselves before bedtime at around midnight, and coyotes across the road were howling wildly. This was a regular occurrence, but this time, the dogs were acting afraid, and then when heavy footsteps were heard right near the house, Tanner got scared too and brought the dogs back inside and told Randy. Randy went outside to listen, but by then, things had grown quiet.

This incident then had a strange offshoot. Tanner had been wearing a hat with a patch on it that said *SF3*. The next day, when Randy went outside, he saw written in the snow right outside the house, *3FS*, the reverse of the symbol on Tanner's hat. What could this mean? I will always be highly skeptical that the creatures understand our alphabet but find it plausible that they can mimic it. The only thing that bothers me here is that they were close enough to hone in on and see the small patch on Tanner's hat. It was a weird incident but in keeping with the high strangeness of the place.

At around this same time, something happened purely for fun and silliness, which, as far as I'm concerned, is always welcome. A collaboration to create a song and music video about Bigfoot occurred between Randy and his band, Smokehouse, the She-Squatchers, and Jason Kenzie as producer. It wasn't a serious emotional ballad but just a fun romp, with Jena Grover as the singer. I'd heard her sing before around the campfire and knew she had a great singing voice, but, my god, she was incredible in this. Randy also had a sax solo, in which he shredded. The video showed a mix of the girls frolicking in the woods, Jena and the band doing their recording at a studio in Bemidji, and a bit of Randy pointing out Bigfoot evidence on his land along with segments of the Minnesota Roars recordings being incorporated. It is titled *Bigfoot Rock and Roar*, and here are the lyrics:

We're journeying into a cryptic woods
Stalking Bigfoot in his own neighborhood
Bigfoot is real, it thrills me to my core
We've gotta find out, we need to know more

Into the woods, the energy shifts
I feel something watching, my mind is adrift
As we search for the red eye that shines in the dark
Just don't pull my arms off or tear me apart

Roaring through the night, something's just not right
Bigfoot is everything all right

When I'm squatching they're watching
Even when I'm snoring they're roaring
I don't wanna be Bigfoot's love slave
So behave

Something's moving behind me, now it's beside me
When I stop, it stops somehow
So Bigfoot it stalking me now

I'm squatching, they're watching
Even when I'm snoring they're roaring
I don't want to be Bigfoot's love slave
So behave

It's silly but so awesome that I'm glad it exists. I also carry pride that it wouldn't exist without me, because, for what's it worth, I introduced Randy and the She-Squatchers.

Randy continued to update me on any new developments he thought were significant in this seemingly never-ending story. Another sighting happened on March 9, 2024. At around 6 PM, which was close to dusk but still light out, he was near his peanut butter gifting area, close to where Jason Kenzie, the She-Squatchers, and myself had found the spiderweb-type stick structure, something Randy had never managed to see for himself, because it was actually gone now. While looking around that area, he saw in the woods about thirty yards away something he had never seen before. It was a large upright figure in the approximate shape of a Bigfoot creature but seeming to be weirdly electronically camouflaged or cloaked—pixelated, as the term goes, much like the alien creatures in the *Predator* sci-fi/horror movie franchise. He had it in sight for only a few seconds. I asked him if he thought it might have been more visible in the dark, but he said no, it was not a matter of lighting. I had read about a similar sighting in the famous Skinwalker Ranch case out of Utah, which had also been compared to the *Predator* films. That called to mind how Randy's place had been referred to by some following his story as the Skinwalker Ranch of the North.

While telling me of this sighting, Randy said he had two recent episodes of what he considered mindspeak while out walking in the woods that had brought clarity to him on a personal level about some of what was going on. But when he described it, didn't seem to be literal voices in his head, but more along the lines of sharply clear ideas just suddenly manifesting. It was about the deer kills and the skulls he had collected over the years. He knew that antlers shed each year by male deer are quickly consumed by various scavengers, yet none of the antlered skulls he'd found showed any kind of chew marks. He'd been thinking that this was because the Bigfoots had left their smell on the skulls, which had repelled any other animals, but now he said this new revelation told a different story. When the creatures killed deer, he said, they were not sitting there and eating them on the spot and leaving the skulls for long periods of time to be found later. Whatever happened to cause the masses of deer hair on the ground was happening quickly, and then the deer's hairless bodies were being taken away out of our dimension to be consumed in whatever realm the creatures originated from. Then the skulls were being brought back to the Earth plane to be left under conditions in which Randy would quickly find them. There were some that he had simply stumbled across as he hiked the woods off trail, and others where he would walk up a trail without seeing anything and then find a skull as he came back the other way—not to mention skulls that turned up near his house or were placed upon deer stands. Randy claimed this information had just been placed into his head by an outside source to help him understand.

Randy's collection of skulls.

I am nearing the point where this writing is catching up to the present, and I think I should include an unexpected contribution to the story. Randy has been in contact with a woman named Robin Haynes McCray, a psychic who claims to have had multiple interactions with Bigfoot creatures over many years and who Jason Kenzie has done documentary filming with in the recent past. She claims not only to be able to mindspeak with the creatures, but also to deduce what each individual's name is. To be honest, I had never thought about Bigfoot creatures having individual names any more than I had thought that about any other type of animal, but Randy said he had been wondering about it and trying to see if he could get them to divulge that information to him but without success. Now that he was in touch with Robin, not in person but over the phone, she said she was able to pick up a certain level of information about his place. I know that a lot of people will not accept this and downright ridicule it, but I have changed my own way of thinking to a great degree since discovering Randy's case, and all I can do is continue to report the information as it continues to come in. Robin said that she picked up on three names of creatures she could see in her mind, two white-haired ones named Darawima and Sushi, and a red one named Ralphafelia. No white ones have ever been spotted on the property, but could the red one be the Big Red that has been seen? She also said there were two families present, and that they represent the Otter Clan, reminiscent of how Native American clans in times past identified themselves with various animals. I have no Earthly idea how to respond to this information except to speculate on how otters are animals that live in and around water and how that might relate to the rivers that wind their way through the area. I have also recently seen a video online about Bigfoot activity in central Minnesota that has no connection to Randy's case in which the presenter talks of how Native friends of his have told him that most Bigfoot creatures have names ending in the letter a, jibing with the names provided by McCray.

Meanwhile, the remote viewing done by the She-Squatchers has also turned up some further details through psychic means. One of the most interesting was Tammy Treichel seeing a mother creature with two little ones and also a young creature spending time and bonding with a mountain lion. This jibes with an earlier experience in which Randy and John Badger had an apparent Bigfoot encounter at night at a tree stand, sighted a mountain lion as they were departing the woods afterwards, then immediately had something throw a log at them. In retrospect, Randy thinks they had probably interrupted a moment between the big cat and a bigfoot, but who can truly say? In spite of the things that seem like sure facts in this case, there is also a ton of room for speculation.

Earlier information on how many creatures might be dwelling around Randy's place seemed to indicate around a half dozen, but psychics have now suggested the number as being as high as twenty.

I don't know. I just don't know. And I really don't know what else to say, except that I am along for the ride in this continuing adventure.

And continue it has. An event occurred in late March, 2024 that gave evidence of the creatures not being just flesh and blood. It had been a mild winter in Minnesota, but now that it was ending, it decided that it wasn't quite ready to give way to spring, and the snow that was nearly melted away kept getting replenished. On the 28th, Randy called me to report that, the night before, there had once again been a pounding on the outside of his house at about 11:30, in response to him having asked for it. This time, however, instead of no tracks being left behind, which had become the norm, there were some. In fresh snow beside the house at the point where the pounding had happened, a total of four footprints were unmistakable. Not a line of them that approached the house and then retreated, but just four. They simply appeared out of nowhere, took four steps, then ended. How can one explain something like this without it being paranormal? Debunkers are likely to say that Randy is a hoaxer and leaned out a window or stood on the roof with fake feet on the end of long poles to accomplish it, but I know him better than that. The prints were smaller than usual, apparently those of a juvenile, he thought, but when I asked him for their exact size, he said he wasn't taking such measurements anymore, because he didn't want the creatures to see him trying to gather evidence on them. Such exact trivialities simply weren't important to him anymore. He did, however, allow me to include a photo of the tracks here, because he wanted the world to see their high strangeness.

Randy has two gifting areas, one that is far out in the state land and one much closer to his fire ring area and his house, where he has constantly been leaving peanut butter jars for the creatures. In this closer area, he leaves many types of items for the creatures to interact with, such as dice, a Rubik's cube, and little blocks of wood that he arranges into various patterns. He regularly finds all of these rearranged. The Rubik's cube would seem to demand an extreme level of dexterity to be manipulated, and I've said that if he were ever to find it completely solved, that would really blow my mind, but that has not happened. He has also left a small white board and magic markers as an invitation for the creatures to write or draw, but that has so far not happened either. He is convinced it is the Bigfoot creatures doing this, though at least one of the psychics that has examined the case has asserted that these intricate little goings on are actually the work of nature spirits that are rooted in the land. They are usually dormant but have been coaxed into being more active because of the presence of the bigfoots. Who can say? If we are going to consider the paranormal, almost anything seems possible.

In the first weekend of May, Randy was in this gifting area and asked the creatures to bend a sapling across a certain trail in such a way that the trail was blocked, the kind of thing he often did as part of his interaction with them. Sure enough, the next day, it had been done just as he'd asked. That same weekend, in his gifting area, the white board had seemingly been stomped on and damaged, the magic marker caps had been removed, and a plastic toy car that had been left there for some time had been torn in half lengthwise. Intrigued by this activity, Randy decided to sit and watch for a while in one of his nearby deer stands, the same one in which he had had a huge creature walk past him in October 2023, so close that he could have touched it.

He was within sight of some apples he had placed in trees, a food that the creatures had always seemed to enjoy, along with oranges and peanut butter—but they showed no interest in bananas or potatoes. As he happened to be looking toward one particular apple, he suddenly saw something he had never seen, something that added even more spectacle to the overall story. The apple, Randy says, suddenly rose up off of the branch it was on and disappeared into thin air before his eyes. What could one imagine but that there was an invisible creature physical enough to be tempted to consume food, standing there snatching it, and then enclosing it in its invisible fist? He had also just found a couple of samples of white hair up to a foot long in that same area, seemingly in keeping with psychics' assertions that there was at least one big white creature present. What normal animal in the American Midwest has hair that long? I suppose one could speculate about the long hair on a cow's tail, but the cows that are pastured nearby are Black Angus. Randy also found a short trackway that weekend—footprints he thought were of a juvenile creature like the ones seen beside the house weeks earlier, but the stride between them was an amazing seven feet.

Randy then had a chance meeting with his friend and past Bigfoot witness, Ron Shaw, who told him that on Thursday, May 2, he had been driving by and had yet another sighting of a large, black, upright creature walking out of a hayfield and then across a gravel road on its way into Randy's property, close to where Randy's wife, Teri, and his stepdaughter, Samantha, had had their own past sightings at the roadside.

On May 29, Randy was by his peanut butter gifting area when he heard branches cracking and thought an animal was approaching, but when he looked toward the sound, he saw something he had never seen. Some branches over twenty feet above ground were breaking and moving as if of their own accord, arranging themselves before his eyes into a neat horizontal structure with two branches perfectly parallel to each other. Though he filmed the structure with his phone immediately after witnessing this, it happened too fast for him to capture the actual moment, but what was he to make of this? Either something invisible had been arranging the sticks, or he had just witnessed pure magic.

In mid-June, Randy's friend and repeat Bigfoot eyewitness, Brian Glynn, attended a psychic fair in Bemidi, where he struck up a conversation with one of the many psychics there about Bigfoot. The lady got such a powerful feeling from him, that she offered to do a free reading for him. During that reading, she seemed to hone in on the creature he had seen on Randy's property, and kind of on a whim, he decided to ask her if she could tell what its name was. After a moment of intense concentration, she answered, "Ralph." This might elicit a laugh or two about the notion of "Ralph the Bigfoot," until one realizes that it harkens back to one of the names provided earlier by Robin McCray—Ralphafelia.

On June 19, I visited the property along with John Badger, and, together with Randy, we went on a typical exploration on a rare nice day during a period when Minnesota had been getting inundated with rain. The rivers were overflowing as never before, and much of the land we usually hiked was under water. We went where we could but didn't find anything of note, and then at night enjoyed the usual time spent sitting around the campfire area. Late that night, as we talked and listened, a faraway noise captured our attention. Though I'd heard several different kinds of vocalizations on the property over time attributed to Bigfoot, I had never heard the famous high-pitched screams that others had, but now, out of nowhere, here they finally were. We walked several yards away from the fire to get away from the sound of the flames to hear the screams as clearly as possible. We simply stood there marveling at them, thinking, no, that's not a coyote; no, that's not a wolf; no, that's not a fox, etc. They seemed to be coming from the approximate location of where a neighbor of Randy's has a cow pasture, and though we'd been hearing the distant sounds of the cows bellowing throughout the night, they were now silent, as if shrinking in fear from whatever this was. The screams went on steadily for three or four minutes and had an erratic quality to them that made me think the screamer must be shaking its head rapidly back and forth. It heavily reminded me of one snippet from the famous Sierra Sounds recording from the early 1970s in California, in which what was taken to be the big male in a family group of Bigfoot creatures was having a temper tantrum, its voice much lower in pitch than we were hearing now but having that same head-shaking sound to it. Then it simply ended, and we were left with one more experience to add to the story. I slept in a tent there that night, but nothing further happened.

On July 28, while out mowing the high grass from some of his trails, Randy saw some things that were new to him, things he did not choose to list among his number of Bigfoot sightings. He thought they were either the "little people" from Native folklore, or maybe the "nature spirits" that some of the psychics talked about. It was two figures he saw, both upright on two legs but only about the size of a raccoon, the first one gray and the second, about an hour later, black. He glimpsed each for only a second or two before they just disappeared, as if he was seeing something by accident that was meant to stay hidden. I asked him if he thought they could have been baby Bigfoots, and he didn't think so.

The next day, as he did almost every day, he visited his gifting area and rearranged some of the many small objects he leaves there inviting the creatures, spirits, and whatever else might haunt the place to come in and interact with them, which, more often than not, does occur with objects getting moved around. It had been suggested by some that the activity might have a demonic nature to it. This was not something Randy embraced, nor did he completely dismiss it. He identifies as a believer in God but does not indulge deeply in Christian practice. On occasion, he had had the dice he left there placed to display the number 666, the ominous "number of the beast," and he had also taken little blocks of wood and fashioned Christian-type crosses out of them, only to have the cross altered the next day. Today, he did this again and asked out loud for the creatures to give him a sign if they didn't like it. He also invited them to bang on his house again that night, which they hadn't done in a while. At about 9 PM that night, the house was banged on, and the next day, the wooden cross was completely destroyed. When he told me about this, I suggested that he try creating symbols of other religions to see if they got the same response, and he said he understood what I was getting at but that, although he felt that he and the creatures were just having fun with these indirect interactions, he didn't want to come across as if he was trying to trick or manipulate them in any way.

Randy is adamant now that he wants to be the one to stand up and proclaim in the face of all popular flesh and blood paradigms among Bigfoot researchers that the creatures are not natural or of this world. He hopes to convince as many people as possible of this while also stating that he isn't hoping to prove it to the whole world but just to gather as much proof for himself as he can and to guide others into doing the same. Proof for the world, he says, is only possible through one person at a time achieving their own personal proof. He is still willing to let certain researchers visit his property, but he no longer puts out trail cameras to try and dupe the creatures into getting pictures of them, and he doesn't want anyone else trying to fool them in such ways either, because they have communicated to him that they don't like it. He feels that he has established a type of friendship with them that he wants to maintain and develop into even more direct kinds of communications. He speaks differently about them now than when I first met him in late 2019. Back then, he said he would never shoot and kill one of them except in self-defense, but now, he firmly believes that no one will ever capture or kill one, because it is impossible due to their paranormal nature. He used to say, "I know a lot about sasquatch, but at the same time, I know nothing about them." He still sometimes says that, but at the same time, he now says, "I don't do speculation. This is my experience. This is what I know."

Here is a chronological listing of the incredible thirty actual sightings that have occurred on and around Randy's property in this case at the time of this writing, which are only part of the whole body of evidence and activity. I will not be a bit surprised if more happens before this book comes out. So that my wording does not become repetitive, all creatures seen are large, hairy, and upright.

1. 2014. While sitting in a tree stand, Randy catches a glimpse of a large creature crossing a trail nearby.

2. June 2014. Chris Cornish, a member of Randy's band, sees a creature in early morning darkness in Randy's yard while sitting outside of the guest trailer. It makes sounds like the Tasmanian Devil cartoon character.

3. November 2017. An anonymous couple, "Junior and Selena,"

who have a hunting cabin near Randy's place, see a big black creature along the highway near his driveway at night while driving.

4. June 20, 2019. Randy sees the nine-foot creature he calls Big Red in the powerline corridor for the first time at close range in daylight. Crouching at first, it stands upright as he approaches but then disappears into the tree line as he glances down. It leaves a handprint in a patch of mud.

5. August 19, 2019. Randy's stepdaughter, Samantha Stomberg, sees a huge dark creature walking into Randy's woods from the highway as she is driving past at night.

6. February 2020. Neighbor Ron Shaw sees a reddish creature crouched in the ditch beside the highway as he is driving past Randy's place. There is deer roadkill nearby that he thinks it is waiting to grab.

7. May 6, 2020. Randy is out walking in the powerline corridor with his granddaughters, Bristol and Madison, when he and Bristol both see a huge black creature, measured as being ten feet tall, standing beside a distant highline pole. Randy loses sight of it when he turns around to make sure the girls are safe, but Bristol sees the creature walk away.

8. July 2020. During a nighttime family outing at Randy's campfire area, one of his grandsons sees red glowing eyes high above ground watching them from beside the nearby deer stand. It disappears as soon as he calls it out.

9. July 18, 2020. Brian Glynn is sitting in a deer stand 100 yards from the campfire area in the evening and decides to come down and go join the group assembled there. As he approaches the campfire, an enormous black figure estimated at ten feet tall comes silently out of the woods and crosses a trail just forty feet in front of him. He is so shocked when he reaches the fire, that he is unable to tell the group what he's seen until after a series of loud screams suddenly bursts out of the nearby woods.

10. August 21, 2020. Randy and John Badger are in a deer stand together at night on the state land near Randy's property when they suddenly see a large rectangular portal of bright shimmering light

about fifty yards away into the woods. Two large orbs of light then emerge from it and float through the air towards where they have placed peanut butter as bait and a trail camera, but there are also footsteps heard along the forest floor. After a moment, they come back along the same path, one still in orb form, but the other one is now appearing in the shape of a bigfoot but still made out of light. They go back into the portal, and it all disappears. The peanut butter is gone, and the trail camera shows nothing, even wiped clean of pictures on it previously.

11. September 19, 2020. During a visit by multiple members of the SRA, during a group hike in the state land, Andy Pieper glimpses a big dark creature nearby in the woods just off trail stand up and disappear behind a rise, seemingly in response to Randy imitating a raven call because of ravens that were circling them.

12. September 19, 2020. That night, while with his son and another man Andy has another sighting while patrolling the trails near Randy's house. They all see a huge dark silhouette estimated at ten feet tall cross a trail very near in front of them as an overpowering foul stench also suddenly strikes them. This happens during a night of intense activity when everyone present experiences something significant, including myself.

13. October 1, 2020. Brian Glynn is visiting and watching from his favored tree stand during daylight while Randy and two other friends, a male and female, are out on a hike. Brian comes down to leave, but when Randy and the other two return from their hike, they see a dark figure in the tree stand, which they assume to be Brian and call out for him to come join them, but they get no response. Only later, do they learn that he had already left, so what was the figure in the stand?

14. The weekend spanning April-May 2021. During another SRA, visit John Badger and another man leave a campfire gathering at night to take a walk around the property. While following the fence line bordering the pasture, John sees a big dark creature emerge from the woods in the pasture in a full-out run, leap over the fence, then disappear back into woods on the other side.

15. May 2021. When Doug Hajicek funds a project to have CCTV cameras installed in the woods near Randy's house, he himself has a sighting on its first night, while watching the live feed from his home, in which three dark creatures walk directly in front of one of the cameras in single file, ranging from six to eight feet in height. Unfortunately, all the settings are not yet complete, and the footage is not captured.

16–17. July 2021. Randy's young granddaughter, Madison, is sleeping on his couch at night and wakes to see a big red-eyed figure looking through the living room window, which leads out on to the second-floor deck, making whatever it is absolutely huge. Her cries wake the house, and in eventual conversation, she reveals that she had also seen another creature on an earlier date through that same window standing out in the yard.

18. October 31, 2021. While walking in the powerline corridor in daylight, Randy sees the big, black ten-foot creature again standing next to the same distant pole where he'd seen it before and vows not to take his eyes off it this time. While trying and failing to get video of it on his phone, he sees it just vanish into thin air.

19. June 2022. Randy's wife, Teri, has her first sighting while driving home from work at night of a huge creature crouched at the roadside near the driveway. It does not flee but just watches the car roll past from only a few feet away.

20. May 2023. During the day, Randy is cleaning out a camper in his front yard when he glimpses something large and black pass by the open door just outside it. No natural explanation accounts for this.

21-22. May 31, 2023. When the She-Squatchers first visit, Jen Kruse and Jena Grover have simultaneous sightings of two different dark figures on either side of the powerline while Randy gives them and myself a tour of the area in the afternoon. They first think they are seeing dead tree trunks, but later, the figures are gone, and by sheer chance, Randy and I have both failed to see them.

23. June 21, 2023. Madison has a third sighting, this time in

daylight, of a big black creature standing at the tree line beside the front yard near the house.

24. August 10, 2023. During the She-Squatchers' second visit, Tammy Treichel sees a dark figure in daylight lean its upper body out of the tree line into the powerline corridor a far distance away, seeming extremely tall.

25. August 11, 2023. The next day, Tammy is standing with me at our campsite near the campfire area in daylight, and as we are waiting for someone to return from an errand, she spies a figure through the brush approaching from a side trail that she assumes is that person, but then no one appears. What did she see?

26. August 11, 2023. Later that same day, near the same area, Jen Kruse glimpses a large dark figure moving through the brush nearby, close to the previous sighting but closer to the river, while I am standing next to her. Noticing the look on her face, I look where she is staring and see a small branch bouncing up and down, but whatever had caused it had just vanished.

27. October 11, 2023. At around dusk, Randy has his closest ever sighting while in a tree stand near his peanut butter gifting area. While struck with sudden dizziness, he hears footsteps in the leaves on the ground and looks up to see a huge Bigfoot head passing by the top of the tree stand, so close that he could have touched it. In comparison to the stand, its height is estimated at 10.5 feet.

28. I have lost track of the date, but at some point in late 2023, neighbor and witness Ron Shaw calls Randy to report that, while driving, he saw a bigfoot walking away from a road into Randy's property.

29. March 9, 2024. Close to dusk, Randy sees, for just a few seconds, a figure in the woods near his peanut butter area that looks electronically cloaked or pixelated, very much like the creature in the *Predator* movies.

30. May 2, 2024. While driving, past witness, Ron Shaw, has another sighting of a large, black, upright creature coming out of a hayfield and crossing a road into Randy's property.

It's an impressive grand total, and shows no signs of stopping. Randy's stepson, Tanner, who has lived on the property for a few years, has had no sightings so far, even though he visits the woods regularly; although, he has had several other types of experiences. I also have yet to have my first sighting there, but I've had the creatures come close to me numerous times. I hope it is leading up to me having that precious lifetime highlight of finally getting to see one. If I do, I can only hope I can stay calm enough to get a photo or video. I've thought that I might also try calling out *Gitche Sabe*, the Ojibwe name for Bigfoot, to see how they respond to that. I learned that name from Jen Kruse of the She-Squatchers, a person I respect and had to atone to for not subscribing to her paranormal views early on. In coming to meet her halfway, it struck me how this iconic and legendary figure of Bigfoot, no matter what its true nature is, and without even trying on its own part, is capable of both bringing people together and of tearing us apart. It seems like a sad commentary.

I was of the opinion that Bigfoot was simply a flesh and blood creature for so many years when I first entered the field. I was well aware that there was a contentious divide between that view and that of others who see them as paranormal. It is Randy's case that has led me—forced me, really—to consider that that other camp just might be right. But as a researcher and author seeking to find common ground among all my fellow Minnesota allies, which is what the focus of this book is all about, I find that I have to stay open-minded to all possibilities. Most Bigfoot reports are of a conventional nature, describing what seems to be just an unusual animal, but then there are those that come from equally reliable witnesses that describe things that can't be taken to be anything other than something super-natural. Is there a compromise that allows me to stay on the fence? I tell myself that perhaps, just perhaps, the creatures are just flesh and blood and part of our natural world, but that there are also para-normal energies and forces that exist in our wild areas that they are intelligent enough to detect and interact with. It's a possibility, one of many.

The screenshot that adorns the top of the page in Randy's Facebook group, showing an orb and possible creature, caught by CCTV camera behind Randy's house in 2021.

Presented in my 2021 book, *Sasquatch Central*, this image still greatly intrigues me. Captured by a trail camera at a deer-kill site on the night of May 14, 2020, when Randy was still using cameras, it shows the back of a massive upright creature some believe to be a bear, and so, it remains officially in dispute. However, the clear crease of the spine, and especially the sharp pointed elbows both pulled far back, make me strongly suspect this is the big black Bigfoot seen by Randy and others.

To speculate further, perhaps there are some creatures fitting the description of Bigfoot that are just flesh and blood and others that are not, and that they are not actually the same thing. There are voices online that warn of this, that there are dangerous things out there masquerading as Bigfoot. Then, too, let us not forget the Native American lore that tells us that Gitche Sabe is a spirit, and always has been. I don't claim to know the truth of all this, but I am dedicated to finding it someday, and I do not believe the possibility of a paranormal nature means ultimate proof is impossible.

Randy's place is a gift that keeps on giving. It takes extreme luck and serendipity for a Bigfoot researcher to find a case like this, in which there is extended and constant activity. Once one does, it takes courage and a leap of faith to present himself to these creatures and attempt to stand toe to toe with them. I am in the process of that in this case. Though they do have their moods and temper tantrums and have caused great fear, they haven't hurt me or anyone else yet, and I don't believe they will. Please wish all of us luck in whatever comes next.

There is no end in sight, and as I said at the end of the last book, the story will continue.

CONCLUSION

In 2019, I produced the book, *Bigfoot Chronicle: A Researcher's Continuing Journey Through Minnesota and Beyond*, which contains every Bigfoot report of every kind that I'd been able to collect, from every available source, in addition to my own contact with eyewitnesses—books, articles, websites, networking with other researchers, etc. The total number was an astonishing 696, and I was correct in predicting then that the number would continue to go higher as new reports came in. That was shortly before I became involved in the Randy Bauer case near Blackduck, which is a phenomenon unto itself. But it's not only there that Bigfoot continues to make itself known in Minnesota, where the number is now well into the 700s.

The Chippewa National Forest in the north-central part of the state has long been known as a Bigfoot hotspot with multiple sightings. Footprints found there, on the Six Mile Lake Road near the little Indian village of Bena, in 2006, brought intense media attention to the area, causing many witnesses to come forward and share their stories. This is not stopping; yet another incident, on October 6, 2023, made its way into the news. On that day, Jeff Stanley and his parents were out grouse hunting along the Six Mile Lake Road system, and as they were driving through the Mud Goose Wildlife Management

Area, they suddenly stopped when they saw a figure standing at the edge of a trail just off the road. Covered in dark hair and with its back to them, at first, they estimated the upright bipedal creature to be about eight feet tall and more apelike than manlike, a classic description of Bigfoot. When the car skidded to a stop and backed up for a better look, the creature slowly turned until it stood in profile, looking at them sideways, not straight on. Then it turned its back again and began to slowly walk away down the trail out of sight. The witnesses were too fearful to go after it. Later in the day, they encountered a game warden on patrol making sure all hunters in the area had proper licenses, and they took a chance and told him what they had seen and exactly where they'd seen it. I have talked to several such wildlife officials over the years about Bigfoot, and their responses have ranged from those who'd seen things themselves, to reluctantly open-minded, to openly dismissive and laughing it off. This warden's response, however, was a surprise. He told the witnesses, "Yeah, that's where people have been seeing them lately." Many thanks to the BFRO (Bigfoot Field Researchers Organization) for thoroughly cataloging this report.

I was able to visit this sighting location shortly after the incident, but the ground was frozen, and there was no evidence to be found. It was exciting though, to know that Bigfoot activity in the area showed no signs of stopping, and that it was so prevalent that even the government seemed to have accepted it as real, though I doubt that will ever become an official position.

Minnesota's place in the roster of Bigfoot habitats has been solidly established, and I have no doubt that reports will continue. It's an exciting time to be a seeker of Bigfoot here, an excitement I share with all my fellow researchers. Though I've been doing this work for nearly forty years, it is striking how my views on the subject have changed so recently. As in all other parts of the country where Bigfoot is seen, the vast majority of reports are of a conventional nature, in which the creatures seen act like flesh and blood animals that, while shocking and mystifying, do not seem to be anything otherworldly. But then there is the smaller percentage of reports made by witnesses who seem every bit as honest and credible as the others who describe things that can only be interpreted as paranormal or even downright supernatural. It is primarily my involvement with the Randy Bauer case that has made me consider this outlook more than ever before; it also makes me reconsider other such stories I've heard in the past.

Is Bigfoot just a flesh and blood animal, whether more closely related to apes or to humans, or is it some kind of paranormal entity? Well, I have long since rejected and abandoned the alternate belief that it is just a myth and doesn't exist at all, but in all honesty, my answer to the question has to simply be that I *don't know*. I have a wide range of beliefs in the paranormal. I believe that UFOs and alien experiences represent the fact that extraterrestrials regularly visit our planet, and also that the dead are not completely lost to us, and that ghosts are not just desperate imaginary things but the literal disembodied souls of deceased human beings. From this mindset, I am left with two possibilities about the reports of Bigfoot being involved with paranormal activity. Either the creatures are paranormal in nature and are literally not of this world and only visit here from some parallel dimension, or they are natural flesh and blood animals who are intelligent enough to detect that there are paranormal energies and forces that exist out in our wilderness areas and sometimes interact with those forces. I know that I am not academically qualified to speak intelligently about such a possibility, but I also know that according to those who work in quantum physics, parallel dimensions and traveling between them are theoretically possible. As I stated earlier, I also speculate about crossovers between the two possibilities that complicate the situation further.

My goal has always been and continues to be to play some role in proving to the world once and for all that Bigfoot is real. If the creatures are paranormal, that would seem much more difficult, but I do not believe that it makes it impossible. I believe that the definition of science should be four simple words: "The Study of Everything." And that that must even include things that do not seem to obey the currently understood laws of nature and physics. "Paranormal" and "supernatural" may be terms for things that are just not fully understood yet.

People see Bigfoot, and that is a fact. Simply calling those people idiots or liars or lunatics is neither fair nor intelligent, and when skeptics brush the phenomenon aside by asserting that there are no bodies, no clear photos, and literally no real evidence of any kind, they are showing that they've done no serious research into the subject at all, because there are truckloads of evidence. There just isn't proof yet. Evidence and proof are two different things. Proof is a level of evidence that is sufficient to establish truth. The phenomenon isn't going away, and the search for that proof will go on. Minnesota is like any other state where the creatures have been reported to exist in that the researchers here are dedicated to the search but divided in their approach to it when it comes to the question of whether Bigfoot is of this world or of some other. Personally, I respect both positions and wish all the luck in the world to both camps as they attempt to validate what so many witnesses have seen and experienced over so many years. I do this work for them; I am one of them, and the adventure will continue.

ABOUT THE AUTHOR

Born in 1967, Michael John Quast is a lifelong resident of Minnesota who grew up on a dairy farm, achieved a degree in Commercial Art, and is employed in a maintenance position for a school system. He makes his home in the city of Moorhead, across the Red River from Fargo, North Dakota.

Since childhood, he has had a deep interest in the paranormal, especially cryptozoology, which was bolstered by his own sighting of a Bigfoot in 1976. Since graduating high school, he has traveled extensively throughout Minnesota, seeking out and investigating Bigfoot reports and exploring wilderness areas in a physical search for the creatures.

He is the author of five previous books on the subject as well as the editor of the former newsletter *Sasquatch Report*.

ALSO BY MIKE QUAST

Bigfoot Chronicles

Bigfoot Chronicles: A Researcher's Continuing Journey Through Minnesota and Beyond

Sasquatch Central: High Strangeness at a Northern Minnesota Homestead

Big Footage: A History of Claims for the Sasquatch on Film

The Sasquatch in Minnesota: Early Minnesota Bigfoot Sightings in The Land of 10,000 Lakes (Bigfoot Chronicles)

AFTERWORD

Go to hangar1publishing.com to learn more about the Authors and stay up to date with their newest releases.

www.ingramcontent.com/pod-product-compliance
Lightning Source LLC
Chambersburg PA
CBHW061750120626
46550CB00005B/1946